# LONDON THEATRE WALKS

*Thirteen Dramatic Tours
Through Four Centuries
Of History and Legend*

## JIM DE YOUNG
### AND
## JOHN MILLER

Photographs by
Nathan Silver

Supplementary photos by Jim De Young

APPLAUSE
NEW YORK • LONDON

*Other Titles from Applause*

**SEATS: 150 Seating Plans to New York Metro Area Theatres, Concert Halls & Sport Stadiums**
Sandy Millman

•

**APPLAUSE: NEW YORK'S GUIDE TO THE PERFORMING ARTS**
Ruth Leon

•

**APPLAUSE: PERFORMING ARTS GUIDE TO LOS ANGELES AND SOUTHERN CALIFORNIA**
Carey Simon

•

**John Willis'
THEATRE WORLD**

•

**John Willis'
SCREEN WORLD**

•

**NEXT SEASON**
Michael Blakemore

•

**THE COMPLEAT WKS OF WILLM SHKSPR (ABRIDGED)**
Reduced Shakespeare Company

•

**FREE SHAKESPEARE**
John Russell Brown

•

**ACTING WITH SHAKESPEARE: THE COMEDIES**
Janet Suzman

•

**MY LIFE WITH NOËL COWARD**
Graham Payn & Barry Day

# Contents

An Applause Original

London Theatre Walks
Copyright © 1998 by Jim De Young and John Miller
ISBN 1-55783-280-3

*Design and Layout by Sue Knopf of Graffolio*

*Library of Congress Cataloging-in-Publication Data*
Library of Congress Catalog Card Number: 98-86923

*British Library of Congress in Publication Data*
A catalogue record for this book is available from the British Library.

**APPLAUSE BOOKS**

211 West 71st Street
New York, NY 10023
Phone (212) 496-7511
Fax: (212) 721-2856

A&C BLACK

Howard Road, Eaton Socon
Huntington, Cambs PE19 3EZ
Phone 0171-242 0946
Fax 0171-831 8478

First Applause Printing, 1998

Printed in Canada

# FOREWORD

These walks have been developed on numerous forays to London over the past twenty-five years. Even though many of the historical places visited no longer exist, we feel that some sense of the past can be captured by knowing you are on the site and by physically coming to grips with the way in which the theatre districts, the theatres, and the theatre practitioners have moved about the city. If you do every walk and visit all the museums recommended, you'll have covered nearly every important theatre and theatrically associated site in central London. At the cost of a bit of shoe leather you should get a concrete sense of just how the various places fit together and how the centers of theatrical activity have moved across the face of the city. To explore Finsbury Fields, Lincoln's Inn Fields, Bankside, Covent Garden, the West End, and the South Bank is to participate in the full sweep of one of the great professional theatre movements of the western world.

Even the casual tourist with an interest in theatre will find the walks a fascinating adjunct to the primary joy of seeing London's high quality live theatre. There is no need to fear you will sacrifice the city's major sights for out of the way corners. Most of the walks follow established tourist routes and will take you by or near places like Trafalgar Square, Piccadilly Circus, the Tower of London, etc.

All care has been taken to make the directions as clear and current as possible, but our warning to you is that landmarks, signs, and even buildings change or disappear rapidly. You should not set out on these walks without a good city map. We personally prefer the *AZ London*, but there are any number available and all will serve if you go astray or wish to truncate or deviate from a route.

Purposefully avoided have been pronouncements on how to pack, where to stay, where to eat, and how to deal with the city. The opening and closing hours of various site or attractions have also generally been omitted as they are often changeable. Things of this nature are best gathered just before you leave for London or immediately upon your arrival.

Reasonable efforts have been made to check names, events, dates, and spellings for accuracy, but some anomalies and certainly some apocryphal stories have crept into the text. Secondary sources can sometimes be wrong or in disagreement. Needless to say we would be more than happy to receive factual corrections, notes on directions that were difficult to follow, and suggestions for new sites to include.

Our recommendation for approaching the walks is to review the titles, read the thumbnail descriptions, and look at the maps. Select those that most interest you and fit in with the other priorities of your trip. If major destinations are a part of any walk, make sure you check current tour times, opening hours, etc. The *Time Out* or *What's On In London* weekly magazines are excellent for that kind of information. For those with access to the Internet, there are several sources for up to date information on London and the London Theatre. Most search engines will locate them with ease.

And finally a grateful thank you to my wife Jan, who has walked every foot of these routes with me, to Glenn Young of Applause Books who never lost faith, and to my co-author John Miller, who moved this project through to completion after a serious illness threatened to turn it into a stillborn child.

*Dr. Jim De Young*
*Director of Theatre*
*Monmouth College*
*Monmouth, Illinois*
*61462 USA*
*E-mail: jim@monm.edu*
*FAX 309-457-2310*

*Note by the British co-author:*

It has taken me more than 40 years of theatregoing in London to complete my tally of all the theatres covered by these walks, culminating in the long-awaited and triumphant opening of the reconstructed Globe Theatre in 1997. I also had the very great pleasure of being present when the other Globe, on Shaftesbury Avenue, was renamed in honour of our greatest living actor—John Gielgud—an occasion for which many of the names mentioned in this book gathered to do him honour. In my collaborations with Sir John on his memoirs for radio, television, and two subsequent books, I have learnt much from his encyclopaedic knowledge of the theatre, and I have endeavoured to add some of that history to these pages. I hope these walks will inspire in the reader the same deep love of the magic of the theatre that has motivated the authors.

*John Miller*
*Author, broadcaster*
*and theatre historian*

# *Break a Blister!*

# WALK ONE

# SHAKESPEARE AND THE GLOBE: A TRIP TO BANKSIDE

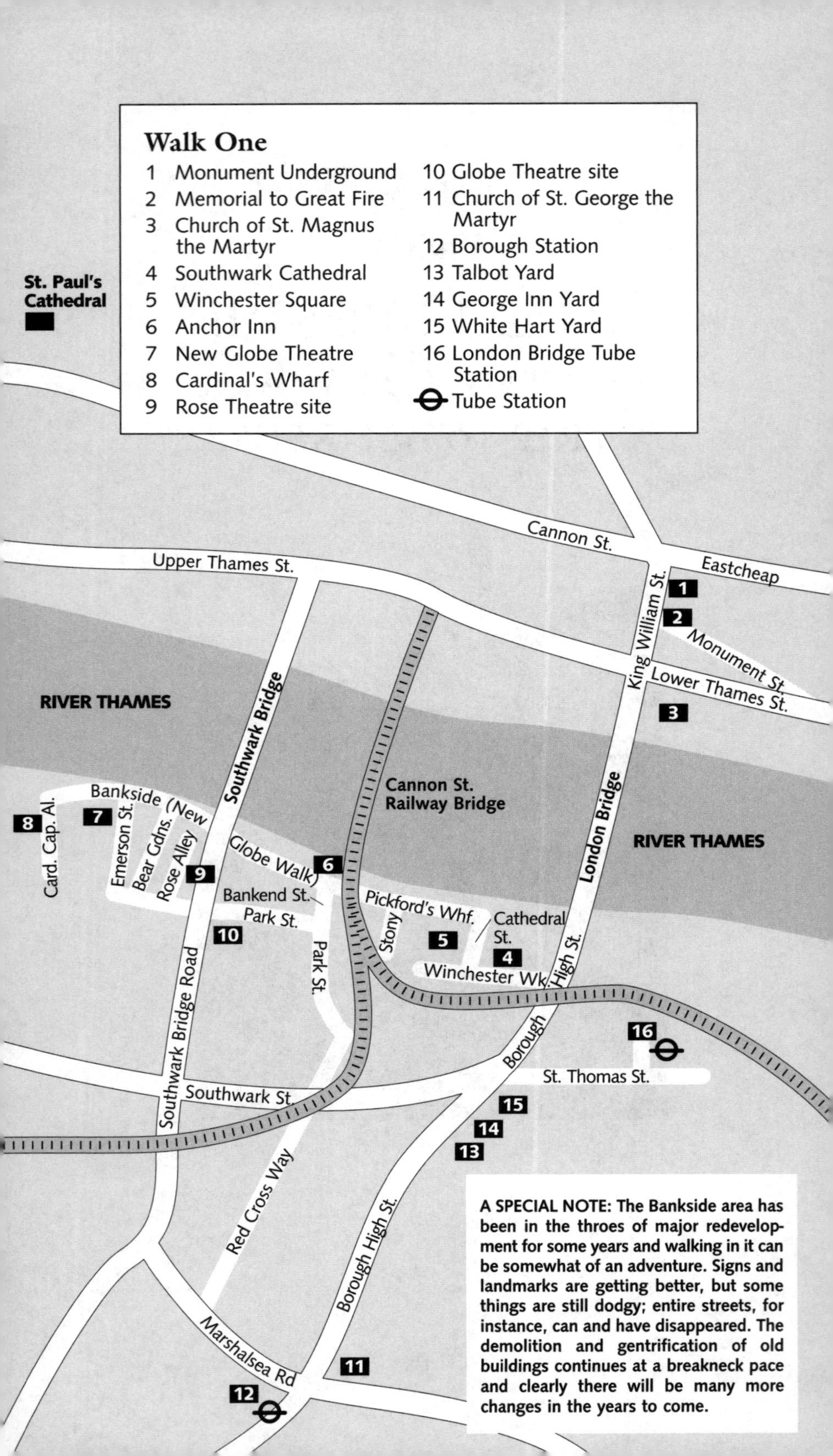

## Walk One

1 Monument Underground
2 Memorial to Great Fire
3 Church of St. Magnus the Martyr
4 Southwark Cathedral
5 Winchester Square
6 Anchor Inn
7 New Globe Theatre
8 Cardinal's Wharf
9 Rose Theatre site
10 Globe Theatre site
11 Church of St. George the Martyr
12 Borough Station
13 Talbot Yard
14 George Inn Yard
15 White Hart Yard
16 London Bridge Tube Station
⊖ Tube Station

St. Paul's Cathedral

Cannon St.

Upper Thames St.

Eastcheap

1

2

Monument St.

King William St.

Lower Thames St.

RIVER THAMES

3

Southwark Bridge

Cannon St. Railway Bridge

Bankside (New

8

7

Emerson St.

Bear Gdns.

Rose Alley

Card. Cap. Al.

9

Globe Walk)

6

London Bridge

RIVER THAMES

Bankend St.

Park St.

10

Park St.

Stony

Pickford's Whf.

5

Cathedral St.

4

Winchester Wk.

Borough High St.

Southwark Bridge Road

16 ⊖

St. Thomas St.

Southwark St.

15

14

13

Red Cross Way

Borough High St.

Marshalsea Rd.

11

12 ⊖

**A SPECIAL NOTE:** The Bankside area has been in the throes of major redevelopment for some years and walking in it can be somewhat of an adventure. Signs and landmarks are getting better, but some things are still dodgy; entire streets, for instance, can and have disappeared. The demolition and gentrification of old buildings continues at a breakneck pace and clearly there will be many more changes in the years to come.

**STARTING POINT:** Monument Underground Station (District or Circle Line)

**APPROXIMATE TIME:** Two hours if you step along, but could take four or five hours if you spend some time at Southwark Cathedral, the Anchor Inn, the Globe reconstruction, and the George Inn. I would personally recommend starting around 11:00 AM in order to take advantage of lunch on the river terrace at the Anchor Inn and an afternoon refresher at the George.

*his walk covers a number of Shakespeare sites and features visits to Southwark Cathedral, two theatre pubs—the Anchor and the George Inn—and the newly reconstructed Globe Theatre.*

Our starting point is the **Monument underground station,** which appropriately happens to be located on the site of the Old Boar's Head Tavern where Sir John Falstaff and Prince Hal gathered with their friends. *Leave the station by the King William Street South exit and turn left toward the new **London Bridge,** dedicated by Queen Elizabeth II in 1973. There's also a sign at the top of the stairs pointing toward the bridge if you are in doubt. The first street on the left is **Monument Street** and it will give you a clear view of **Christopher Wren's memorial to the Great Fire of London.*** There's no theatrical connection there, but if you have a driving desire to climb 311 stairs as a warm-up for a two-mile walk you might wish to take a short side trip. *Otherwise continue down **King William Street** toward the Thames.*

*As the bridge approach gains height you cross over Lower Thames Street. Look down and to your left for a view of Christopher Wren's church of St. Magnus the Martyr.* Its rather pleasant little steeple is now literally pasted up against an office block. *Shed a quiet tear for this sad little edifice and then cross out onto London Bridge.*

You may still see its predecessor about 10,000 miles to the west. It was taken apart stone by stone and reassembled as a tourist attraction in Lake Havasu, Arizona. But the bridge of theatrical interest is neither of these. It is instead the great medieval bridge that was

**Christopher Wren's memorial to the Great Fire of London**

completed in the year 1209 and stood for over 600 years. That bridge stood a bit downstream (towards Tower Bridge) from where you now stand. If you look at a current street map, think of it as more in line with Gracechurch Street. During Shakespeare's day both sides of the bridge were lined with shops and stores and at the Southwark end was a gatetower on top of which was displayed, like so many martini olives on toothpicks, the severed heads of executed traitors and criminals.

In January of 1599 theatrical history moved across that bridge. When James Burbage and his brother-in-law built the first public play-house in England in 1576, they called it The Theatre and put it up on leased ground in Shoreditch (see Walk Eight). When the lease expired in 1597 Richard and Cuthbert Burbage, who took over their father's affairs after his untimely death, could not renegotiate satisfactory terms and The Theatre was forced to close. The acting company apparently moved their main performance base to the nearby Curtain Theatre. In 1598 a decision was made to invest in a new theatre on the south bank of the Thames. A thirty-one-year lease was conveyed to a group of so-called "Housekeepers" of the Chamberlain's Men. Half of the lease was in the names of the two young Burbage brothers; the other half was split five ways among a group of actors—John Heminge, Augustine Phillips, Thomas Pope, William Kempe, and William Shakespeare.

In December of 1598 or January of 1599 The Theatre was torn down and the timbers transported along Shoreditch High Street, up Bishopsgate and Gracechurch Street, over the old London Bridge, and into the parish of St. Mary Overie, now known as Southwark. There the lumber was used to erect a fine new playhouse called the Globe. The actual location was upstream of this bridge and is now hidden from your view by other bridges and buildings.

But let's not get too far ahead in our story. *As you cross London Bridge, to your left you will see Tower Bridge—the roadway between its twin towers is raised whenever a large ship needs access to the Pool of London. Cross over to the right hand side of the bridge to approach London Bridge now and somehow (this is no easy task, believe me) get to the right hand side of the road at the site of the infamous Thames river stairs where in Dickens' Oliver Twist Nancy is overheard by Noah Claypole telling the secrets that will lead to her murder by Bill Sikes.*

*Beyond the river steps and just before the railway bridge new signage clearly points the way into the* **Southwark Cathedral churchyard** *and toward the new* **Globe Theatre.** The yard is a space that William Shakespeare would have recognized and its age is advertised by the fact that you literally go down to its level from the modern streets. *As you walk through it you pass first the most ancient parts of the cathedral, the 13th century choir and retrochoir; then the 15th century transepts; then the 16th century tower; and finally the Victorian nave, which was reconstructed to the original Gothic plan in 1897.*

The interior of Southwark Cathedral is usually open throughout the day. Access is of course limited during services. The church has a fine organ and is also the site of lovely lunchtime and evening concerts. Special programs in honor of Shakespeare are usually held on or around the Bard's birthday in April of each year.

*After entering the cathedral stand at the rear of the nave.* There is no proof that Shakespeare was a regular visitor here, but we do know that he lived nearby for some time and that he did enter the church at least once. On December 31, 1607, the sexton's accounts include this entry: "Edmund Shakespeare, a player, buried in the church with a forenoone knell of the great bell, 10s." Of Edmund Shakespeare, William's younger brother, we know only that he was baptized in Stratford in 1580 and was buried in London in an unknown spot in this church. The critical thing about the sexton's note is the total of 20 shillings for the funeral. It cost only two shillings to be buried in the churchyard and only one shilling for a tolling of the small bell. Most sources agree that brother William must have been the purchaser of this costly obsequy.

Two other theatrical people, the Jacobean playwrights John Fletcher (1579-1625) and Philip Massinger (1583-1640) are also buried, reputedly in the same vault, somewhere in the church. Fletcher is perhaps best known for his collaborations with Francis Beaumont, e.g. *A Maid's Tragedy* (1611), but he also worked with Massinger. A good half of Massinger's forty plays have been lost and he is chiefly remembered today for one satiric comedy, *A New Way to Pay Old Debts.* One or both of these men are thought to have collaborated with Shakespeare on *Henry VIII* and *Two Noble Kinsmen.*

Philip Henslowe ( -1616), the theatre manager and builder whose diary is a source for much of our knowledge of Elizabethan theatre practice, is also buried here. Both he and his associate, the actor Edward Alleyn, lived within the parish and served as vestrymen in the church for a time.

*If you now stroll down the south aisle of the nave (this is on your right if you are facing the altar), you will soon find the Shakespeare Memorial Window and Monument.* The rather romantic alabaster statue of the reclining bard dates from 1911, while the window was completed in 1954. It features a galaxy of Shakespearean characters, with Prospero the old magician, arms raised, holding court at the center. See how many of the rest you can identify. (The answers are listed at the end of the walk so you can check your responses.)

**1**

Scenes from Southwark Cathedral, clockwise from top left:

Detail of Shakespeare window

Entrance

Shakespeare statue

Sam Wanamaker plaque

Exterior

*You can retrace your steps and leave the cathedral now, but if you continue on around the church to visit the retrochoir and transepts you will find several outstanding tombs, including that of John Gower—a good friend of the poet Geoffrey Chaucer. Stop to look at the models of the old church and especially the Bishop of Winchester's Palace. Keep them in mind when you leave. The Harvard Chapel is also worth a look, as is the marvelous collection of old medieval roof bosses.*

*As you leave the cathedral you'll pass a recent memorial to a group of young people killed in a disastrous Thames boat accident that occurred in 1989. Exit the building, turn right and mount the few steps out of the churchyard.* What was a deserted Dickensian warehouse district in 1975, and a construction site throughout the 80's, is now a thriving, gentrified business and commercial area. *Straight ahead of you lies* **Winchester Walk**. *Take it. If you look right at the first street you will be looking into old Winchester Square.* Nineteenth century buildings, most of which are now gone, used to literally preserve the shape of the courtyard in front of the palace of the Bishop of Winchester. Remember that model or the relief back in the church of the Southwark skyline above the reclining figure of Shakespeare.

Since it was both convenient and politically prudent for bishops from provincial cities to have a dwelling available near to the seats of power in Westminster and the City of London, it was common for them to take land near the City and literally annex it to their own diocese, thus making a real home away from home. The manor or park surrounding the Bishop's palace, some seventy acres in this case, was therefore a little piece of Winchester or what was known as a "Liberty" area. A "Liberty" was simply a parcel of land within a city that was exempt from the laws of the city because it was not legally a part of the city. In this case the city was the City of London and the City had definite proscriptions against certain types of public entertainment. Thus most professional Elizabethan theatre activity took place in "Liberty" areas within and/or around the fringes of the City.

*Now reverse your course and go back toward the Cathedral. Turn left at the first chance. This is* **Cathedral Street** *and it will take you under a skywalk and toward the river. Off to the right is the new chapter house of Southwark Cathedral.* Sales of riverfront property in recent years have financed the building of a new chapter house complete with lavatories and a restaurant. *As you approach the river you will see a reconstructed trading schooner (which can be toured for a fee). Dead ahead is a new pub and a paved court with a pleasant river overlook enhanced by signage that identifies most of the buildings visible on the far shore. Explore these attractions for a bit if you wish. When you are finished turn around and walk back away from the river next to the pub and look for the first narrow street on your right. It is labeled* **Pickford's Wharf**.

*Walk for a few yards down Pickford's Wharf and keep your eyes alert on the left for what looks like an excavation site. At the far end of the*

**1**

*diggings is a wall complete with a striking remnant of an old stone rose window.* The remains were first exposed in 1814 when a mustard factory on the site burned down, but they were covered up by 19th century warehouses. World War II bombing exposed them again and later

excavation has identified the fragments as parts of the Bishop of Winchester's 13th-century Great Hall. The openings low down on the west wall led to the kitchens, the domestic quarters, and the cellar. The window itself was apparently inserted into the existing wall in the 14th century.

We know that the Bishop gave a great banquet in this hall in 1604 to celebrate the accession of King James I to the throne of England and Scotland. We also know that a procession of great splendor preceded the affair. Might the procession have given Shakespeare's theatre company, the newly named King's Men (who formerly were the Chamberlain's Men) a chance to show off some of their freshly drawn livery from the Royal Wardrobe? (See Walk Two for more details on this event.) Might

**Remains of Bishop of Winchester's Great Hall**

we even suppose that some of the talented neighbors from the Globe Theatre just down the way entertained at that banquet?

*Continue walking now on Pickford's Wharf.* This actually used to be called Clink Street and it was an Elizabethan theatrical enclave. Philip Henslowe, Philip Massinger, Francis Beaumont, and John Fletcher all had lodgings on this street. *You'll shortly arrive at the intersection of **Stoney Street** coming in from the left. The open space that appears to be a kind of rubbish tip cum car park used to be the kitchens of Winchester Palace.* Excavations on the site in 1965 turned up vast quantities of oyster shells and other assorted debris from long forgotten meals. Some old walls are still visible at the far end of the lot and may be from the kitchen or as now claimed from the Clink prison. (An older sign used to designate the prison as about 200 yards further along Clink Street.)

Wherever the Clink Prison was, we are certainly close to it here. It was in this jail that the Bishop of Winchester incarcerated heretics and ne'er-do-wells (including some of the Pilgrim Fathers). The use of the term "clink" for jail probably originated here. Some say the name literally came from those outside who heard the clink of the chains from within.

*As you move on past the vacant lot into the narrow unmarked opening that is all that remains of the Dickensian Clink Street, you will see the entrance for a tourist attraction operating out of a basement and called "The Clink Prison Museum." Give it a pass unless you are really hard up for cheap thrills.*

*Keep walking and you will shortly plunge under the forbidding arch of the* **Cannon Street railway bridge.** *As you emerge back into the light you should be able to see the* **Anchor Inn.** A tavern has stood here since the 15th century and the site is not more than 200 yards or so from the original location of Shakespeare's Globe Theatre. The current tavern fabric, which dates from the 1750s, has seen several additions and renovations in this century and even though its charm may be a bit spurious, its clientele a bit citified, and its prices a bit dear, it's still worth a wander around. Stay out of the restaurant upstairs unless you are not on a budget. Rather grab a pint and a snack from the bar and head for the riverfront terrace. On a sunny afternoon there may be no better place in town from which to enjoy London's

**View of the Thames from the Anchor Inn Terrace**

greatest highway—The Thames. It takes no imagination at all to see Shakespeare and his fellow players as patrons of this inn or one like it. We definitely know that Dr. Samuel Johnson, the great 18th century author and lexicographer, was a regular patron of the Anchor. He had rooms on Park Street in the home of Mr. Thrale, a brewer.

*After a suitable rest and refreshment, pass along the river on what is now known formally as* **Bankside.** *You will shortly come up on and then pass below* **Southwark Bridge.** *You will find yourself still on Bankside and walking now in front of a building called Riverside House. At the first left turning possible* **(Bear Gardens),** *low on the wall of Riverside House and just around the corner is a small piece of Elizabethan England that was there when Shakespeare walked this street.* It is an old Thames Ferryman's Seat, a resting spot for one of the many boatmen who took pleasure seekers across the rive to taste the many delights of Bankside.

*Don't turn into Bear Gardens now. We'll be back in just a short while. Continue walking along Bankside (now renamed New Globe Walk). Just past the next left, which is* **Emerson Street,** *you will see Sam Wanamaker's* **new Globe Theatre** *reconstruction.* The building is not actually on the site of the real Globe, but it's close enough for government work. A preview season featuring a production of Shakespeare's *Two Gentlemen of Verona* opened in late August of 1996; the

9

**1**

Scenes from the New Globe

1

**Scenes from the New Globe**

**1**

formal grand opening took place in June 1997. Two of the four plays in the first season were by Shakespeare: *Henry V* and *The Winter's Tale*; the others were Middleton's *A Chaste Maid in Cheapside*, and Beaumont and Fletcher's *The Maid's Tragedy*. The mythology of the new Globe is already beginning to form. The opening production was not "The Scottish Play" but apparently an actor fell and broke his leg during the first preview. How's that for taking the theatre's universal good luck wish literally? In any case, when you arrive you should arrange to take a building tour, visit the museum displays, and book some tickets if possible. The sheltered seats in the galleries are more expensive, but the standing-room in the open for "the groundlings" is more fun, and evinces much more audience involvement. Sam Wanamaker, an indomitable American actor, director, producer, and entrepreneur, spent more than twenty-five years of his life trying to bring this dream to a reality. Please give it your full support and attention.

*After you have exited the theatre, make your way once again to the banks of the Thames. Find yourself a spot on the pleasant riverside wall, face the river, and try to picture this scene as it may have looked in 1600.* On both sides, stretching out along the bank, would have been rows of decrepit houses of prostitution called "stews." The women in these houses were sometimes called "Winchester Geese." Remember, we are still in the Bishop of Winchester's Liberty area. Of course there was also a liberal sprinkling of tawdry taverns and ale houses. Behind them would have been the high outlines of the theatres and bear baiting rings. Across the Thames, then as now a busy commercial waterway, could be seen the majestic bulk of St. Paul's Cathedral. Shakespeare would have been looking at the old St. Paul's, a Gothic church which was longer and about one hundred feet higher than Sir Christopher Wren's building. Before lightning struck it and burned

**New Globe Walk**

the tower in 1561, Old St. Paul's spire reached 489 feet into the air. The current St. Paul's tops out at a paltry 365 feet.

*Now move down New Globe Walk a little further and look for a small group of older buildings on your left. A large gas lamp on one of them signals the entrance to tiny **Cardinal Cap Alley**—one of London's narrowest streets. The cream-colored 17th century house, labeled **Cardinal's Wharf**, has been named by some sources as the home where Christopher Wren stayed while he was building **St Paul's**. If it wasn't it should have been, for the spot gives you a picture postcard view of the great cathedral.*

*If the gate is unlocked, plunge down narrow Cardinal Cap Alley. After you have moved a few steps in, turn back, and get an even more splendid view of St Paul's. Continue on into the alley a bit further. Note how the pavement rises and then falls. You have just crossed an old Thames flood barrier. Keep going until you are almost to the end of the alley. Listen for the sound of birds and look for a small wooden door almost covered with vines on your left. Bend down and peek through a tiny screened hole. You might just catch a glimpse of a wisp of a garden complete with singing birds and fishpond—a tiny little secret Eden tucked away in a most unlikely spot.*

*Return to Bankside, turn right and walk past the Globe to Emerson Street, turn right on Emerson and then left on **Park Street**.* In Shakespeare's day it was called Maid Lane, and this is the street on which the Globe and the Rose Theatres actually fronted. *A short block will bring you to **Bear Gardens**.* Just down this street

Cream-colored house is Cardinal's Wharf. The little arch immediately to its right is Cardinal Cap Alley.

was located the Bear or Paris Gardens. Philip Henslowe held a controlling interest in the building and used it for animal baiting up to 1613. He then demolished it to make room for the Hope Theatre (1614-1656) where Ben Jonson's *Bartholomew Fair* was first performed. Six years after the destruction of the Hope, the Davies Amphitheatre (1662-1682) was built on the same site. It was once visited by Samuel Pepys and mentioned in his diary.

*Continue your walk down Park Street, which is not well-marked until you near Southwark Bridge Road. The next crossing on your left is Rose Alley, or what is left of it. In the basement of a new building for the*

**1**

*Financial Times, on the right hand side of the alley moving along toward the bridge, encased in sand, and sealed below a lid of cement, lies the remains of the Rose Theatre.*

The Rose was the first public playhouse on Bankside and was built by Philip Henslowe around 1587. The Lord Admiral's Men played there until the Fortune Theatre was built in 1600. It was demolished around 1605. In 1989 Dame Peggy Ashcroft, then aged 81, led an actors' protest against developers' plans to build over its foundations, and at one point stood in the path of the bulldozers and defied them to drive over her. This spirited campaign by one of the great ladies of the theatre forced Imry Merchant to spend £10 million on redesigning an office on stilts, to preserve these historic foundations which reveal so much about the Elizabethan layout of stage, tiring-rooms and so on. If you wish to know more about The Rose, its recent discovery, and the fight to preserve it, check out *The Rose Theatre* by Christine Eccles.

*Continue down Park Street. You will shortly cross under **Southwark Bridge Road**. As you come out from under the bridge, note the tower of Southwark Cathedral coming into view.* It is once again a sight that William Shakespeare would have recognized. And indeed you are now almost on top of the site of the most famous theatre in the world. *Archaeologists have located pieces of the Globe in the basement of Anchor Terrace just to your right. The Terrace has recently been rebuilt as a block of smart apartments. Stop and read the display panels in front of them, which contain interesting information about the original Globe Theatre.* More of the theatre is also apparently underneath the road itself. Thus there seems little chance of further archaeological research in the near future. You are about as close as you are ever going to get to the spot where the timbers dragged from The Theatre in Shoreditch were reassembled in 1599.

So take the image of the Globe reconstruction you have just seen and see if you can imagine yourself standing right here waiting for admission to the theatre on opening day in 1600. The tower of Southwark Cathedral tower would have been clearly visible in the distance. You should also remember that there were two Globes, not one. The first Globe burned in 1613 (ignited apparently by a piece of flaming wadding from a cannon fired during a production of *Henry VIII*) and was replaced by a similar structure on the same foundation in 1614. The second Globe lasted into the 1640s. Even though a large portion of the output of the world's pre-eminent dramatist was first performed here, we have never known very much about the theatre itself. The surviving exterior views of the playhouse (mostly from maps of the period) are not the same and there is no extant interior view at all. Results from the most recent excavations (at the Globe and the Rose sites) seem to have resolved some of the knotty problems surrounding the nature of Shakespeare's Globe, but there is still plenty of uncertainty left for the scholars of the 21st century.

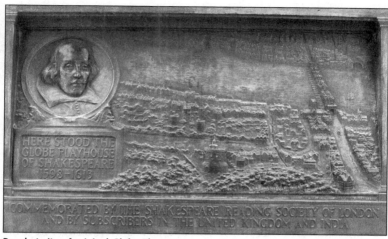

**Panel at site of original Globe Theatre**

*We have now reached the culmination of our walk. If the flesh is weak or the hour is late, you can continue down Park Street to a tee junction. A left turn on* **Bankend Street** *will lead you quickly back to the* **Anchor Inn** *and from there you can retrace your steps back to* **Southwark Cathedral** *and through the Cathedral precincts and up the stairs to the busy* **Borough High Street.** *You can then either turn left and walk back across the river to the Monument tube station where you started or cross Borough High Street and walk up the street opposite until you get to the entry to the* **London Bridge tube station** *on the Northern Line.*

*If the spirit does remain willing and you wish to see the last remaining galleried coaching inn in London, take the right turn at the tee intersection, which is the continuation of Park Street. Follow this as it makes a gentle curve to your right and then a curve to the left. Just before a railroad overpass, turn right on* **Red Cross Way.** *Shortly you will reach a major road with more bridges crossing overhead (***Southwark Street***). Head directly across the street for an arch that is a continuation of Red Cross Way. Follow this narrow street all the way to* **Marshalsea Road.** *It will take you through a quite dingy though typical working class neighborhood, past a school, some cottages set back from the street, and some council flats. Turn left on Marshalsea Road for a block to reach Borough High Street.*

*As you reach the High Street the* **Church of St. George the Martyr** *is almost directly across from you and the* **Borough station** *on the Northern Line is just to your right. Cross the street to reach the church.* In its graveyard is buried a true theatre curiosity in one Mr. Nahum Tate (1652-1715). His claim to fame rests on his 17th century improvements of Shakespeare. Under his hand *Richard II* is reworked and titled *The Sicilian Adventurer.* Tate's version of *King Lear* omits the Fool and has Cordelia survive to marry Edgar. Lear also remains alive to give

**1**

away the bride. What is even more unbelievable about all this is that Tate's adaptation of *King Lear* remained the standard acting edition until the early part of the 19th century, when William Macready finally restored the original text. If all of the above seems faint praise, you might prefer to remember Tate as the composer of the lovely Christmas carol, "While Shepherds Watched Their Flocks by Night."

*After a brief look at the church (if it is open), a right turn (assuming you are exiting from the front door) onto the Borough High Street will set your course back toward London Bridge. If you are heading the right direction Tabard Street should be just ahead of you.* The middle of the High Street (they are high because the Romans actually raised them for better drainage and you are indeed walking on a Roman road) marks the site of the old Marshalsea Prison where Ben Jonson was incarcerated for sedition in 1597 and where Charles Dickens' father was imprisoned for debt. The young Dickens lived nearby with his family while his father was in the prison. *Shortly on your right you will come upon the John Harvard Public Library.* It appears to function as a socially active neighborhood center and often has nice exhibits of Borough history. It is well worth a look if you are interested in the ambience of real British life as opposed to the servicing of the tourist industry. Read the bulletin boards. Fascinating!

*As you continue down the High Street you will come upon a string of tiny alleyways, some closed off and some open.* Each of them used to lead to one of the many coaching inns that lined this main route into and out of London. *There is Queen's Head Yard, which was the site of an inn owned by the family of John Harvard and sold by them before they emigrated to America. After a bit of a walk you will curve slightly and be able to see the railway bridge next to Southwark Cathedral. Talbot Yard is just a short distance on and is the site of the famous Tabard Inn where Chaucer's Canterbury Pilgrims launched their famous journey. The next opening is the George Inn Yard and it must be explored for inside is the last remnant of a galleried coaching inn in London.* The facade dates from 1676-77 and its plain narrow rooms with crooked floors and low ceilings definitely recall an earlier day. Occasionally in the summer Shakespearean plays are performed in the courtyard. New construction on two sides in the yard has removed some of the sense of age that used to be there but at least the balcony motif has been carried on.

With some more of that old imagination we have called upon so often, you should be able to see from this fragment how suitable the old inns would have been for drama. Some scholars believe that this is the main architectural model for the permanent Elizabethan theatre. It would have had controlled access, a place for a stage at one end, places for patrons to stand, galleries for the more affluent, convenient spaces for actors' dressing areas, and refreshments on the premises. It is easy to see how an enterprising professional with a bit

George Inn

of capital could find an advantage in an arrangement that would reproduce the same basic physical space without the necessity of paying rent to an innkeeper for use of the yard. Other advantages are also quite obvious. The stage could be left in place and used for rehearsals, there would be permanent storage for costumes and props, the producing company could set its own admission prices, and most importantly, the income from food and drink sales would swell the company's coffers and not the innkeeper's.

Art aside, the reality check here is quite clear. The Elizabethan theatre of William Shakespeare and his colleagues was above all a competitive, professional, commercial enterprise. The times were hard, the margins narrow, and you had to use every edge you could find.

*Enjoy some refreshment or just reflection at the George Inn, then return to the Borough High Street and turn right toward the river once again. The very next opening is* **White Hart Yard** *and the site of the old White Hart Inn.* This was the rebel Jack Cade's headquarters in Shakespeare's *Henry VI, Part 2.* In Act IV Cade's forces fight their way across London Bridge to Cannon Street (you walked under the Cannon St. railway bridge just before you got to the Anchor Inn a while ago) and then make plans to storm the Tower, the Savoy, and the Inns of Court. But by Scene Eight of the play Cade has fallen back to Southwark again and in a parley with Buckingham and Clifford speaks to his own wavering forces, "Hath my sword therefore broke through London's gates, that you should leave me at the White Hart in Southwark?" Several centuries later the White Hart was still an inn and Mr. Pickwick first met Sam Weller there in Dickens' novel, *Pickwick Papers.*

**1**

*You are now almost back to the river. You can turn right just before the railway bridge over the **High Street** and find the **London Bridge tube station** (It's still in Zone 1 and on the Northern Line), or continue straight on back over **London Bridge** and return to the **Monument station** (Circle and District Lines) where you started.*

**Quiz answers to help you identify the Shakespeare characters in the memorial window at Southwark Cathedral:**
*(See next page.)*

Left panel from top down—Puck and Bottom from *A Midsummer Night's Dream,* yellow cross gartered Malvolio making his love appeal to Olivia while Maria eavesdrops from the bushes in *Twelfth Night,* then Sir John Falstaff, then Portia in her law garb, "The quality of mercy is not strain'd," etc. from *The Merchant of Venice,* the contemplative Jaques sitting in the forest of Arden from *As You Like It,* and the Fool from *King Lear.*

Bouncing up to the top of the center panel you should see three characters from *The Tempest*—the sprite Ariel soaring over the figure of Prospero while Caliban crouches below.

At the top of the third panel you can see young Romeo and fair Juliet in the balcony scene, then Richard II holding in his hand the hollow crown, then Richard III, King Lear, Othello, Lady Macbeth, and finally Hamlet with the skull of poor Yorick.

Across the bottom of all three panels from left to right is Jaques' famous "Ages of Man" speech from *As You Like It.*

> All the world's a stage,
> And all the men and women merely players.
> They have their exits and their entrances,
> And one man in his time plays many parts,
> His acts being seven ages. At first the infant,
> Mewling and puking in the nurse's arms.
> Then the whining schoolboy, with his satchel
> And shining morning face, creeping like snail
> Unwillingly to school. And then the lover,
> Sighing like furnace, with a woeful ballad
> Made to his mistress' eyebrow. Then a soldier
> Full of strange oaths and bearded like the pard,
> Jealous in honor, sudden, and quick in quarrel,
> Seeking the bubble reputation
> Even in the cannon's mouth. And then the justice
> In fair round belly with good capon lined,
> With eyes severe and beard of formal cut,
> Full of wise saws and modern instances;
> And so he plays his part. The sixth age shifts
> Into the lean and slippered pantaloon
> With spectacles on nose and pouch on side,
> His youthful hose, well saved, a world too wide
> For his shrunk shank; and his big manly voice,
> Turning again toward childish treble, pipes
> And whistles in his sound. Last scene of all,
> That ends this strange eventful history,
> Is second childishness and mere oblivion,
> Sans teeth, sans eyes, sans taste, sans everything.

1

Memorial window at Southwark Cathedral

# WALK TWO

### ❀

# WILLIAM SHAKESPEARE

## AND THEN SOME

### FROM CHANCERY LANE TO BLACKFRIARS

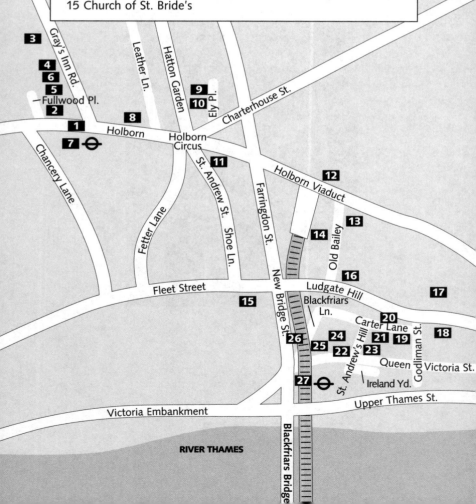

## Walk Two

1 Chancery Lane Station
2 Cittie of York
3 Gray's Inn Gardens
4 Gray's Inn Square
5 South Square
6 Gray's Inn Hall
7 Staple Inn
8 Furnival's Inn Site
9 Church of St. Etheldreda
10 Mitre Tavern
11 Church of St. Andrew
12 St. Sepulchre Without Newgate
13 Old Bailey
14 Magpie & Stump
15 Church of St. Bride's
16 St. Martin's Within Ludgate
17 St. Paul's Cathedral
18 City of London Information Center
19 Site of Bell Inn
20 Dean's Court
21 Wardrobe Place
22 Cockpit
23 Church of St. Andrew by the Wardrobe
24 Blackfriars Monastery site
25 Playhouse Yard
26 Blackfriars Pub
27 Blackfriars Tube Station
⊖ Tube Station

**STARTING POINT:** Chancery Lane Station (Central Line). Note: The station is closed on Sundays, but only attempt this walk Monday through Friday, as the Inns are all closed on weekends.

**APPROXIMATE TIME:** Two hours with minimal stops and three hours if you include the lunch hour and some breaks along the way.

*T**his walk begins at an interesting pub, visits several locations associated with Shakespeare, two Inns of Court, a few fascinating churches, some historic theatre sites, and finishes at a marvelous Art Nouveau pub that was designed and decorated by a member of the Royal Academy.*

*T*ravel *on the Central Line to the **Chancery Lane tube station**, and once at the top of the escalator ascend the Holborn North Side stairs. Once at street level, walk along for about 100 paces past the #7 High Holborn Building toward the large beckoning clock of the **Cittie of York pub.*** Plan to arrive here right about noon in order to take advantage of some pub grub. If you arrive later than 12:15 you may find the crowds of lawyers intimidating.

The Cittie of York is one of the most venerable and intriguing of London pubs and a popular gathering spot for Gray's Inn lawyers. The first alehouse on this spot appears to date from 1430. The current building dates from 1695 and was rebuilt using some of the original materials in 1923. The front of the pub was remodeled extensively in 1983, but if you go through into the rear of the bar you will see some older and rather impressive-looking wine vats above your head. They were actually used as late as 1940. On the whole this cathedral of pubs seems an ideal place to start our journey through this part of William Shakespeare's London.

**Cittie of York**

**2**

*So order up a pint of hand drawn bitter and some hearty food to tide you through an afternoon of hard walking. If you have arrived early enough you might be able to get one of the little private booths, which were constructed so that lawyers could discuss their business discreetly during lunch.*

*After you finish your lunch, leave the pub, turn right, and then turn right again in about fifty yards at a small gatelike passage called* **Fulwood Place.** *If you become aware of* **Chancery Lane** *coming into the street on your right, you've missed Fulwood Place and should turn around and walk back a bit.* As you enter the archway you are walking into the precincts of Gray's Inn, one of the four London Inns of Court. The four Inns (Gray's, Lincoln's, the Middle Temple, and the Inner Temple) date from the 13th century and exist to provide office space for lawyers and to provide lectures and certificatory examinations to students wishing to qualify for the bar in Great Britain.

*Follow the passage until you reach lovely* **Gray's Inn Gardens.** They were a favorite strolling place for ladies of good and ill repute throughout the 17th and 18th centuries. There used to be two aged catalpa trees up at the far end of the garden that were supposedly planted by Sir Francis Bacon from slips given to him by his friend Sir Walter Raleigh, who had brought them all the way from America. Unfortunately age or disease took their toll sometime between 1988 and 1992 and they have disappeared. Garden strolling used to be limited to Inn members but these days, whatever your repute, you may sample the delights of the greenery from 12:00 to 2:30 PM (May 1 to September 30 only).

*If you go into the garden, return to the gate where you entered and turn left when you exit. If you don't go in, turn right and walk along the edge of the fence looking ahead of you for a tunnel-like opening labeled* **Gray's Inn Square.** *Go through the tunnel. The square is on your left as you emerge.* The most famous resident here was Sir Francis Bacon who lived at No. 1 Gray's Inn Square for almost fifty years. Bacon (1561-1626) was the foremost intellectual and essayist of his time. He has even the distinction of having been nominated by some as the true author of William Shakespeare's plays.

The prize for the most infamous Gray's Inn theatrical connection must go to the Anglican clergyman Jeremy Collier (1650-1726). Collier made his black mark on theatre history when he published his *Short View of the Profaneness and Immorality of the English Stage* in 1698. When not involved with church affairs or attacking the evils of the Restoration theatre, Collier was a law lecturer at the Inn. Other theatrical residents were the Elizabethan dramatist Thomas Middleton (1570-1627), who was a student at the Inn, and the 18th century dramatist Oliver Goldsmith (1730-1777), who had lodgings within the Inn precincts. Goldsmith was buried at the Inner Temple and we visit that site in Walk Five.

**2**

*Unless you wish to stroll in the square proper, turn immediately to your right and proceed down the lane toward the* **South Square.** *The building on your left is* **Gray's Inn Hall.** It dates from 1560, although it and several other buildings in the area had to be extensively rebuilt after World War II bomb damage. During the 15th and 16th centuries students at the Inns of Court provided some of the best audiences for live drama and the Inn halls were ideal locations for performances. Records indicate that William Shakespeare's *Comedy of Errors* was given its first known performance in Gray's Inn Hall in 1594. Unfortunately the hall is still used as the Inn's dining room today and entry is restricted. For some fascinating discussion of the nature and arrangement of performances in the halls of the Inns of Court, you might like to look at Robert Burkhardt's article in *Theatre History Studies* Vol. XII, 1992.

*Return now to* **High Holborn** *using the archway on the opposite side of the square from the hall. As you emerge turn left. Walk along past the tube entrances. On your right across the street is* **Staple Inn,** an Elizabethan facade that escaped the Great Fire of London in 1666 by a fortuitous wind change. (Walk Three starts at Staple Inn and you can find more information on the building there.)

*Cross over* **Gray's Inn Road** *and continue walking now on* **Holborn.** *Shortly on your left you will pass the red brick Victorian Gothic bulk of the Prudential Assurance Company. It stands on the site of* **Furnival's Inn,** *where Charles Dickens stayed while writing the first part of* The Pickwick Papers. The playwright James Barrie of *Peter Pan* fame also lodged at the Inn for a short time.

Gray's Inn Hall

**2**

*Cross over **Leather Lane** and start looking for a street called **Hatton Gardens,** which should come up on your left.* This street, now the center of London's diamond trade, is named after Sir Christopher Hatton, Elizabeth I's Lord Chancellor and also her favorite dancing partner. Hatton was apparently no one else's favorite but the Queen's, but in those days that was the one favor that counted.

*We will rejoin Hatton himself in a moment, but for now walk by Hatton Gardens and bend slightly to the left at the **Holborn Circus** spaghetti bowl. You'll find yourself on the beginning of **Charterhouse Street**. Almost immediately on your left will be the gates of **Ely Place**.* This cul-de-sac roughly defines the former palace of the Bishop of Ely. It has been a "liberty" area, and therefore outside of city jurisdiction, since the 13th century. To this day it is privately guarded at night and in theory not even the metropolitan police can enter uninvited. *As you enter the enclave it might be interesting to note that from 1600-1624 the Bishop's old palace served as the residence of the Spanish Ambassador to England and during that time one of the last medieval Passion Plays done in England was performed in the house.*

*But our real interest here is at the back left corner of the close where you will find the enchanting church of **St. Etheldreda**. Walk there now, go in, and climb the stairs to the sanctuary.* This church, formerly the

Bishop of Ely's private chapel, is all that remains of this once elegant complex. All, that is, except some interesting memories out of the plays of William Shakespeare. The Bishop's gardens, for instance, were apparently quite well known. In *Richard III*, the Bishop of Ely is a character and Richard, the Duke of Gloucester, says to him: "My Lord of Ely, when I was last in Holborn, I saw good strawberries in your garden there; I do beseech you send for some of them." The residents of Ely Place continue to commemorate this event with a strawberry festival held each year during the last week of June.

**St. Etheldreda**

26

The Bishop's Banqueting House also made a footnote for itself in history. Henry VIII and Catharine of Aragon attended a five-day feast there in 1531. The menu has been preserved and consisted of 24 beefs, 100 muttons, 51 veals, 34 porks, 10 dozen capons, 13 dozen swans, 340 dozen larks, and as the centerpiece, a whole ox.

**2**

*The church of St. Etheldreda has always been one of my favorite spots in London. Take a seat and look about you.* It is a 13th century Gothic building of livable proportions whose major claim to fame is that it was the first pre-reformation English church to be returned to the Roman Catholics, and it is claimed that the chapel at West Point in the United States is patterned after this church. Even though the building escaped the Great Fire of 1666 as a result of the same wind change that saved Staple Inn, it has still been much restored. Major work occurred in 1870, 1935, and again after the second World War. The 500-square-foot west window (modern glass) is one of the largest in London, and the chestnut roof is simply superb. Gracing the sides of the walls are painted life-size statues, not as you might expect of great saints, but of ordinary people who rose to martyrdom by sheltering priests or failing to take the oath of supremacy in the dark days of the 1530's. Look particularly at the figure of John Roche, a Thames waterman, and Anne Line, a seamstress. It may be the gentle gazes of those quiet, little known martyrs, or the soft aroma of incense and melted candles, but the sanctuary somehow seems to incorporate and reaffirm their personalities and their faith. It is all that a church should be. Please leave a generous gift in one of the collection boxes. This is not a money gouging tourist venue.

*When you leave the sanctuary make your way back down the ancient stairs and look for the crypt entrance on your left.* This space, now a serenely simple chapel, rests on Roman foundations. John of Gaunt, the famous Lancaster, father of Henry IV and brother-in-law of Chaucer, who came to live at Ely Palace in the late 1390s, died in the palace in 1339 and his mortal remains may have reposed for a time in this very crypt. The circumstances surrounding his death were immortalized by William Shakespeare in *Richard II,* Act II, Scene 1. In that scene Gaunt speaks of his country in as eloquent a manner as has ever been spoken. He says:

> This royal throne of Kings, this scepter'd isle
> This earth of majesty, this seat of Mars,
> This other Eden, demi-paradise:
> This fortress built by nature for herself
> Against infection and the hand of war;
> This happy breed of men, this little world;
> This precious stone set in a silver sea
> Which serves it in the office of a wall
> Or as a moat defensive to a house,
> Against the envy of less happier lands:

This blessed plot, this earth, this realm,
This England!

*With the congenial resonance of those words in your ears, step back outside into Ely Place once more.* It is time to pick up the story of Christopher Hatton again. In 1576 Queen Elizabeth was seeking a way to reward her good friend Hatton and thought that some choice Holborn real estate might be ideal. She asked the Bishop of Ely to lease most of his house and grounds to Hatton for a yearly rent of 10 pounds, 10 loads of hay, and one red rose from the garden. The Bishop demurred and the Queen sent a note that said, "Proud prelate, you know what you were before I made you what you are! If you don't immediately comply with my request, by God, I'll unfrock you." The Bishop, being a practical man, rapidly signed the lease. Hatton got his estate, but later got into financial difficulties, fell from the Queen's favor, and ultimately died a broken man.

Mitre Tavern

*Walk now down the right hand side of Ely Place (west side). A bit more than half way back to Charterhouse Street is a small opening in the facade of row houses. It is about four feet wide and has a narrow iron bar down the center of the opening to make it even narrower. It is called Ely Court and you should turn right into it. In about fifty paces this tiny alley will reveal one of London's best hidden pubs. It is the splendid **Mitre Tavern** that dates from 1546.* What you see now, though, is the product of an 18th century renovation. The site of the tavern is supposed to mark approximately the division between Christopher Hatton's garden and the Bishop's remaining piece of garden. *Filled with this historical tidbit and perhaps an additional libation of old English bitter, step back out onto Ely Court, turn right, and continue on until it pops out into Hatton Gardens. Then turn left and walk back out to Holborn Circus at the jaunty hat-tipping statue of Queen Victoria's beloved Prince Albert.*

*Once at the Circus ignore Charterhouse Street, which would lead you back to Ely Place, and choose instead the wide **Holborn Viaduct**. Just across from you is the grey stone of the **Christopher Wren church of St. Andrew.*** The great fire of 1666 had just reached and destroyed the old church when that sudden change of wind referred to a few paragraphs ago came up and saved Ely Place, Staple Inn, and other buildings on High Holborn from destruction. St. Andrews was destroyed again by the Germans in 1940 and it was not until the 1960s that his fine building was completely restored to its 17th century glory. Should you wish to visit the interior you will find that William Hazlitt, the Shakespearean critic, was married in the church in 1808. Charles Lamb and his wife were best man and bridesmaid. Both men lived nearby on Southampton Buildings.

*Your route will now take you across the* **Holborn Viaduct,** *which represents one of the many truly great large scale Victorian engineering projects that altered the face of London.* The viaduct is over 1400 feet long and carries traffic over the ancient "stream in a hollow" (Hole Bourne) portion of the now buried Fleet River. For hundreds of years this valley had been a major bottleneck for horses and wagons attempting to enter the city through Newgate. Finally in 1869 cast iron came to the rescue and the long hill was no more.

*Holborn Viaduct will give way to your next landmark on the left which is the tower of* **St. Sepulchre Without Newgate,** *topped by four small spires.* This church goes back to the 12th century, but has been remodeled and restored many times since then. Some of the current interior work is by Christopher Wren. It is open only on Wednesdays from 12 to 2.

Americans may wish to step inside the church to see the grave of Captain John Smith of Pilgrim fame. It is located in the south aisle. Theatre enthusiasts may wish to see the famed Newgate execution handbell that was sounded outside a condemned man's cell on the night before he was to die. It was given to the church in 1605 and is alluded to in Act IV, scene 2 of John Webster's *The Duchess of Malfi.* The executioners have arrived in the room and Bosola says to the Duchess, "I am the common bellman, that usually is sent to condemned persons the night before they suffer." William Shakespeare also knew of the bell. He would have passed the old church each time he came from Stratford and entered the city through the Newgate. In Act II, scene 1 of *Macbeth* he has Lady Macbeth say, "Hark! Peace! It was the owl that shrieked, the fatal bellman which gives the stern'st good-night." St. Sepulchre is also well known today as the musicians' church and is the site of excellent and varied noon hour concerts.

*Diagonally across the way from the church stands the grey mass of the Central Criminal Courts Building or as it is more commonly known,* **The Old Bailey.** The corner itself is the site of the old Newgate into the city of London. The gate was large enough to include a prison and it was there that the Elizabethan playwright Ben Jonson was incarcerated after killing Mr. Gabriel Spencer in a duel. It was also where Christopher Marlowe was jailed for suspicion of complicity in a murder. Newgate's real theatrical fame, however, lies in John Gay's *The Beggars Opera* (1728). The entire play is set in and around old Newgate Prison and its vivid picture of London lowlife in the early 18th century is unmatched anywhere. The escapades of Macheath, Lucy Lockit, and Polly Peachum climax with the tolling of an exe-

**2**

cution bell (from St. Sepulchre). Bertolt Brecht and Kurt Weill's *The Threepenney Opera* (1928) with its famous title song "The Ballad of Mack the Knife" was based on Gay's play.

In 1783, after a disastrous fire, the architect George Dance designed another and larger prison for the site—a structure that was called "a prototype of Hell" by Henry Fielding. If you wish to soak up some of that building's atmosphere, one of its original cells is on display in the Museum of London. Up until 1774 it had been common for prisoners in the old Newgate to be transported to the Tyburn Gallows for execution. Clergymen from St. Sepulchre were traditionally on hand to give each condemned person a nosegay and a blessing as they rumbled by. As late as the 1890s the church bells were rung to mark executions at Newgate itself. If you'd like to pursue the grisly history of these prisons, I'd recommend a book titled *The Triple Tree: Newgate, Tyburn, and Old Bailey* by Donald Rumbelow.

*At the end of the church, cross* **Holborn Viaduct** *and start down* **Old Bailey Street** *with the Criminal Courts Building on your left. Once on Old Bailey Street you may notice a sign on the new building to your right for the* **Magpie and Stump public house.** The current pub is at least the third on the site. Legend has it that a last drink from the Magpie's pumps was offered to all condemned prisoners from the old prison and that the landlord sold upper window seats to the wealthy so they could have a better view of the execution in the square outside. The 19th century Magpie and Stump was severely damaged in 1973 by a powerful explosion that was attributed to the Irish Republican Army. The pub was literally destroyed and every single window in the high rise building ahead of you was blown out; you can still pick out some pockmarks and patched areas from the blast on the walls of the Criminal Courts Building.

*About halfway down the length of the building is the doorway where you enter if you wish to observe a London criminal trial.* Check out the times if you want to see some real modern English drama.

*Otherwise continue to move down Old Bailey Street toward the intersection with* **Ludgate Hill.** *New construction in recent years has erased several interesting features so you'll have to do some imaginative reconstruction as you walk.* First imagine that you are really walking along the banks of that same invisible river you just crossed on the Holborn Viaduct. Fleet Lane (named after the Fleet River) used to cut off to your right and run steeply downhill toward the railroad tracks. At the bottom of Fleet Lane was Seacoal Lane. During the late middle ages ships brought high quality coal down the coast from Newcastle (Yes, that's the origin of the phrase 'It's like bringing coals to Newcastle.'), up the Thames, and finally up the Fleet River. They tied up along Seacoal Lane to unload their cargo. Alas, just a modern and terribly uninteresting office block now.

*A short stroll further and you will be at the intersection of Ludgate Hill. In the distance off to the right you should be able to see the tiered wedding cake levels of Wren's beautiful church of St. Bride's, which we visit in Walk Five.* This intersection is now packed with traffic and tourists, but it is a lot more circumspect than it was in the 1500s. At that time it was a downright unpleasant corner of the city. The Fleet River was a fetid open sewer, the coalyards contributed a layer of grime, and there were at least two prisons in spitting distance of where you are standing. Right in the middle of all this was the infamous Belle Sauvage Inn. Records indicate that companies of players used the inn for performance in the 1570s and 1580s. Richard Tarleton, the most famous of Elizabethan clowns, and most probably the model for the king's jester referred to by Hamlet when he says "Alas, poor Yorick, I knew him, Horatio," played at the Belle Sauvage shortly before he died in 1588. The inn was still embroiled in "evil" theatrics over forty years later when in 1632 William Prynne (1600-1699), a zealous puritan residing not far away at Lincoln's Inn, published his *Histrio Mastix,* a ferocious 1000 page attack on actors and the theatre. One passage refers to the profane playing at the Belle Sauvage of a play called *Faustus,* which featured an actual appearance by the devil. Mention is also made of some audience members who were sorely frightened by this apparition. Luckily for us the old inn is now long gone and no apparitions have been reported by the chartered accountants who currently inhabit the area. If you are in the mood for a light hearted treatment of this old superstition and an actor's life around the old Elizabethan innyard theatres, look up Edward Marston's delightful murder mystery titled *The Merry Devils.*

*Turn left now at Ludgate Hill and begin your climb toward the grand dome of St. Paul's Cathedral, passing on the way the Wren Spire of St. Martin's Within Ludgate. You may of course stop and visit St. Paul's at this time if you wish, but our walk today is merely going to go by the building and plunge immediately into the precincts of Blackfriars.* Walk Five, "A Fleet Ramble to St. Paul's," formally culminates with a visit to this magnificent symbol of the city of London.

*When you reach the open space in front of the St. Paul's Cathedral, edge your way off to the right toward the round City of London Information Center. Turn to your right at Godliman Street just in front of the tourist office, then go about thirty paces down Godliman Street and turn right again into Carter Lane. Watch carefully on your left now for the sign for Bell Yard and just below it to the right a small dirty white plaque that marks the site of the Bell Inn.* On October 25, 1598, Richard Quinney of Stratford-Upon-Avon was staying at the Bell Inn. He was in a bit of a financial bind and penned a letter to another Stratford fellow who was doing right well for himself in London. Quinney's letter is the only known piece of private correspondence addressed to William Shakespeare. It begins, "To my loving and good friend and countryman, Mr. Wm. Shakespeare," and then asks the successful playwright for a 30-pound loan. There is no record of Will's

**2**

response, but it couldn't have been too negative, as some years later Quinney's son married Judith Shakespeare, Will's eldest daughter.

*A bit further along on Carter Lane is **Dean's Court** where the Dean of St. Paul's Cathedral lives. Just beyond is an extraordinary mock renaissance palazzo that used to house the St. Paul's choir school and is now a youth hostel. Watch closely on your left now as you walk for the narrow arched entrance to **Wardrobe Place,** another of those hidden spots that* make London a delight to explore. There is no street sign, just a small metal plate saying No. 1 Wardrobe Place. If you arrive at a street called **St. Andrew's Hill** before you find Wardrobe Place you've gone too far and should go back and look again.

St. Paul's Cathedral

Once in the small shady yard, put your imagination cap on again. Wardrobe Place was the site of the King's Wardrobe where, from the time of Edward III (14th century) the robes of state were made up and stored. In 1604 on this location William Shakespeare signed a receipt for 4½ yards of cloth to be used to make livery for the state entry of James I into London. Shakespeare's company, the Chamberlain's Men, had been invited to become the King's Men after Queen Elizabeth's death and were now entitled to wear royal livery. If you have taken Walk One, you may recall that we mentioned this episode in connection with the possibility that Shakespeare's company might have shown off their new livery at the great celebration at the Bishop of Winchester's palace on Bankside to honor the accession of James I.

*Turn left after you leave Wardrobe Place and proceed the few steps to **St. Andrew's Hill.** Turn left again and walk down the hill.* The narrow streets are graphic reminders of London's past. This district was burned to the ground in the great fire of 1666 and Christopher Wren's initial rebuilding plans called for wide open streets radiating from St. Paul's. The grandiose ideas never quite made it off the drawing board and ultimately the buildings were rebuilt following the medieval street plans. Thus you walk today through twists, turns, and narrow alleys that would have been totally familiar to Shakespeare and his fellow actors. City planners are once again arguing these questions. World War II bombing destroyed much of a similar rabbit warren of streets on the other side of St. Paul's. The sterile office blocks that were erected in the 1950s are already looking a bit shabby. The Prince of Wales, who has made the despoiling of London by faceless modern architecture one of his royal crusades, has referred to this part of the city as a sad example of what can happen when commercial interests take precedence over historic and aesthetic interests.

*A little over half way down St. Andrew's Hill on the right hand side of the road is the* **Cockpit public house.** Its decor today recalls the 16th century venue that used to occupy the space. William Shakespeare would certainly have known the cockfighting parlor that stood here, for he had a home somewhere within a hundred yards of where you are now standing. On March 10, 1613, Shakespeare purchased a property known as the Blackfriars Priory Gatehouse on Upper Thames Street. The signed deed can be seen at the British Museum. It may have been purchased because of its closeness to the Blackfriars Theatre, where the King's Men played during the cold winter months when the open air Globe across the river was closed.

*From your vantage point you can also see ahead of you and slightly to the left the entrance to the* **Church of St. Andrew's by the Wardrobe.** *Just in front of the Cockpit, on your right, is a small alley called Ireland Yard. Turn into this passageway and walk down it until you come to a tiny courtyard on your right containing three trees fighting for life amid the surrounding brick walls. Walk in for a moment. You are now in the confines of the* **Blackfriars Monastery,** *a religious community that occupied this area as early as the 13th century.* There was a church, a cloister, a priory, various outbuildings, and even a dock down on the river. At one point, during the tenure of Sir Thomas More as speaker, the English Parliament actually met within the walls of the Priory.

After Henry VIII dissolved the monasteries in 1539, the grounds were held by various nobles as so called "Liberty" areas, which were free from City of London control even though they were within the bounds of the city. In 1548 the precincts were granted to Sir Thomas Cawarden, who was then the King's Master of Revels. Cawarden rented out parts of the complex for dwelling and business purposes, but also allocated some space to acting companies of young choir boys. More on this in a moment.

*Exit the courtyard now, turn right, and step along a little further on Ireland Yard. You will soon come to a slightly larger space called* **Playhouse Yard.** Somewhere near this spot a small monastery building was adapted for theatrical use by Richard Farrant and the Children of the Chapels' Royale. This was the first Blackfriars Theatre. Performances by these young choir boys were popular among court audiences and seem to have been given regularly from 1576 to 1580. Other boys' companies used the space periodically over the next years, but by 1584 it was being let out for lodgings. In 1596 James Burbage, builder of London's first public theatre in Shoreditch (The Theatre—1576), leased another small hall nearby with the idea of converting it into a theatre. Even while remodeling was in process, there were complaints lodged against the appearance of professional players in the district. The boys' companies had close court ties and were considered to be innocent and genteel amateurs whereas the boisterous and unruly professional players were not thought to be positive influences on neighborhood ambience or property values.

Just before the remodeling was finished James Burbage died. The Burbage heirs (sons Richard and Cuthbert) decided not to push the question of professional playing in the precinct any further at that time. They finished the work and leased the building to another boys' company, which played there until 1608.

In 1608, James I formally disbanded all the Boys' Companies and the building was left without a tenant. Two years later Richard Burbage, William Shakespeare, and four other King's Men shareholders negotiated a new lease and received permission for adult professionals to use the space. The King's Men used this Second Blackfriars Theatre from October to May while returning to the Globe for the summer season. It appears that the King's Men retained possession of the building until the formal closing of all theatres in 1642. A quick look at a map can also tell you just how important the location of this building is. An indoor theatre with a small capacity needs to charge more for seats and thus circumscribes its clientele. The Blackfriars was close to the various Inns at Court and the string of Royal, Ecclesiastical, and Ducal Palaces that ran along the Thames from Westminster to the Tower. For the full story of this remarkable venue see Irwin Smith's *Shakespeare's Blackfriars Playhouse.*

*Opening off to the right from Playhouse Yard is yet another narrow alleyway called Church Entry. Cross into it and not far along on the left you will discover a more deeply buried but actually quite pleasant little courtyard that used to be the graveyard of St. Ann's Blackfriars, the parish church of the Blackfriars Priory.* Some sources indicate that the church, which bordered closely on the Blackfriars theatres, sometimes had its services disturbed by the sounds of trumpets, uproarious cheers, and loud drums emanating from performances.

*Step back out of the old graveyard and continue on up Church Entry until you emerge once again into **Carter Lane**. Turn left and stroll along until you reach a tee intersection, which is **Blackfriars Lane**. Turn left and follow its winding course down to Queen Victoria Street.*

*My choice for end-of-walk refreshment comes just after you turn right off Blackfriars Lane onto Queen Victoria Street. Walk under the railroad bridge and look on your right for the distinctively shaped Blackfriars Pub, decorated inside and out in 1903 by Henry Poole of the Royal Academy.* It is an Art Nouveau masterpiece. There has been a pub on the site since 1600 and the current one, with its marble, bronze, wood, and mosaics, is worth a visit by any standard—Shakespearean or otherwise.

*After your libation a subway just outside of the door of the pub will take you under the street. **The Blackfriars tube station** (District and Circle Lines) awaits your tired feet.*

# WALK THREE

# LINCOLN'S INN FIELDS
## AND ITS ENVIRONS

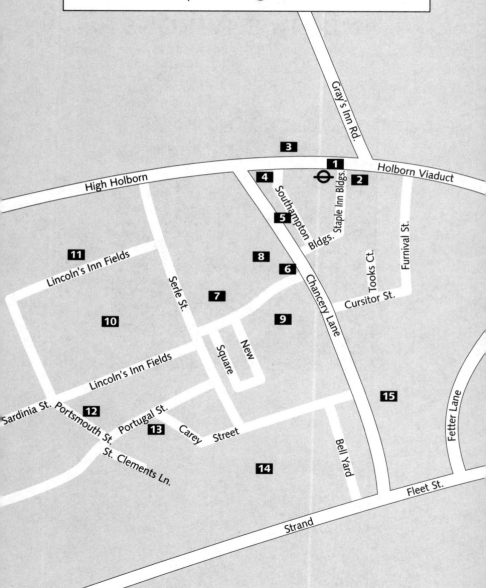

# Walk Three

1 Chancery Lane Station
2 Staple Inn
3 Gray's Inn
4 Southampton House
5 London Silver Vaults
6 Lincoln's Inn Gate House
7 Lincoln's Inn
8 Lincoln's Inn Chapel

9 Old Square
10 Lincoln's Inn Fields
11 Sir John Soane Museum
12 Old Curiosity Shop
13 Lincoln's Inn Fields Theatre
14 Law Courts Buildings
15 Public Record Office
⊖ Tube Station

Gray's Inn Rd.

Holborn Viaduct

High Holborn

Southampton Bldgs.

Staple Inn Bldgs.

Furnival St.

Chancery Lane

Tooks Ct.

Cursitor St.

Serle St.

Lincoln's Inn Fields

New Square

Lincoln's Inn Fields

Fetter Lane

Sardinia St.

Portsmouth St.

Portugal St.

Carey Street

Bell Yard

St. Clements Ln.

Fleet St.

Strand

**3**

*T*his walk contains some important Restoration the-atre history and features as its centerpiece a visit to the Sir John Soane's Museum. This incredible pri-vate home is not to be missed by any serious student of art, architecture, or theatre. There is also a possible visit to the London Silver Vaults. Since the Soane Museum visit is a crit-ical part of this walk, you may want to double-check the cur-rent opening hours, usually 10-5 Monday through Saturday.

Y*our starting point is the **Chancery Lane tube station** on the Central Line. Exit the station by the **Holborn** South Side stairs. You will come up right alongside **Staple Inn**.* This is one of the very few original half timbered frontages left in London. The name has designated a gath-ering place for wool staplers from as early as the 14th century. The term "staple" was used to classify the quality of cotton or wool—indi-cating that it was of fine, long or short "staple." In the 15th century the legal profession began using the Inn and it soon became an offi-cial Inn of Chancery whose function was to feed young legal trainees into the advanced courses at nearby Gray's Inn or Lincoln's Inn.

What you are actually looking at here is only a much restored facade, but it does date from 1568, which qualifies it as one of the few pre-

Great Fire views left in London. Since we know that William Shakespeare visited the Great Hall at Gray's Inn and the nearby home of his patron, the Earl of South-ampton, we can con-fidently assume that he would still recognize the view today.

**Staple Inn**

37

*A few feet farther along is a gateway. Turn right between Whittard's Tea and Sanford's Jewellers. Look carefully at the huge doors and make sure you read the sign underneath the arch as you pass through. You will now find yourself in a pleasantly restored 18th century court-yard.* Should you be captivated by it you are in the very best of company, for it has been weaving its magic for some time. Charles Dickens described it this way in his novel *Edwin Drood:*

> [It] . . . imparts to the relieved pedestrian the sensation of having put cotton in his ears and velvet soles on his shoes. It is one of those nooks where a few smoky sparrows twitter in the smoky trees, as though they called to one another, let us play at country.

*At the rear and to the right in the courtyard is located a fine little Elizabethan hall dating from 1580, which now belongs to the Society of Actuaries.*

*For an even more pleasant surprise penetrate into the second court-yard. There you will come upon an enchanting jewel of a garden complete with gurgling fountain and a rainbow of flowers.* Here indeed is one of London's secret spots visited only by those who know where to go to escape the noisy ravages of city traffic. Even in winter the spot has a certain charm. Nathaniel Hawthorne, the 19th century American novelist, also visited Staple Inn and finding himself in the inner court, where you now stand, wrote in his journal:

> There was a surrounding seclusion of quiet dwelling houses, with beautiful green shrubbery and grass plots . . . and a great many sunflowers in full bloom. . . . I have a sense that bees were humming in the court, though this may have been suggested by my fancy, because the sound would have been so well suited to the scene . . . . In all the hundreds of years since London was built, it has not been able to sweep its roaring tide over that little island of quiet.

*When you are fully refreshed leave the inner courtyard of Staple Inn via the short flight of stairs at the back gate. The first street on the right is **Southampton Buildings**. Henry Wriothesley, the young Earl of Southampton, lived with his mother in **Southampton House** just up the way where **Chancery Lane** blends into **Holborn**.* We do not know exactly how Shakespeare met Southampton, but we do know he was one of the Bard's early and major patrons.

That Shakespeare was a regular visitor at Southampton House we can also be assured; he may even have lived there in 1593 when the plague closed the theatres. Will's first printed work, the long poem titled Venus and Adonis, was dedicated to Southampton and some scholars believe that Southampton inspired many of the Sonnets as

**Staple Inn second courtyard**

well. It is also thought that the premiere performance of *A Midsummer Night's Dream* was given in the great hall of the Earl's house on May 2, 1595. If that's not enough for this one little street, we can also note that in much later times the Shakespearean critics Charles Lamb and William Hazlitt both lived on Southampton Buildings.

*You want to go straight ahead at this point as turning right would put you back out onto Holborn. Keep looking at the building entrances on your right for a small sign that says "The London Silver Vaults."* Inside and down the stairs is enough sterling silver to keep the Lone Ranger in bullets for a lifetime. This side trip has nothing to do with theatre, but the vaults are well worth a visit; some of the items are priced quite reasonably. *If you do not wish to cross your palm with silver, proceed straight ahead until Southampton Buildings terminates at **Chancery Lane.***

*Directly across from you now is **Lincoln's Inn**, one of the four London Inns that educate, certify, and provide office accommodation for the British legal profession. If you go about 100 yards to your left you will see a venerable Tudor gatehouse, which was restored in the reign of George V.* Some of the money to construct it was given by King Henry VIII. The playwright Ben Jonson, Shakespeare's friend and contemporary, is said to have worked as a mason on the gatehouse when he was a young man. *Enter the Inn by the gate and walk into the first court. Tyrone Guthrie and his wife had their first London home in the attic of No.23 Old Buildings, which is to your left.* They lived there for many years from early in the thirties until the middle fifties, when he was doing much exciting and pioneering work with the Old Vic Company, including Olivier's Freudian *Hamlet* in 1937, and Ralph Richardson's *Peer Gynt* in 1944. He later founded the Stratford Ontario Theatre

**Tudor gatehouse
of Lincoln's Inn**

and the Guthrie Theater in Minneapolis. The quirky little flat figures often in the Guthrie mythology. *Walk on through the first court, bending a bit to your right, so you are walking along the open undercrofting of the **Lincoln's Inn chapel**. Stop for a moment before moving through the arch ahead of you.*

Lincoln's Inn is the oldest of the four Inns of Court and its formal record books go back to 1422. The name comes from Henry de Lacey, the 14th century Earl of Lincoln, who once owned some of the land on which the Inn stands. *A bit to the left is the Old Hall, which was built sometime between 1490 and 1520.* Sir Thomas More spent a good deal of his professional life there. Its most famous fictional use was the setting for the opening scene of Charles Dickens' *Bleak House:*

> And hard by Temple Bar, in Lincoln's Inn Hall . . . sits
> the Lord High Chancellor . . . ; and before him is the great
> cause, never to be understood, of Jarndyce vs Jarndyce.

*A large arch, separating the Old Hall and the Chapel, will pass you into the **old square**. If the chapel is open, you may wish to pay a visit.* It was built in the 1620s, perhaps to plans by Inigo Jones. The dedication sermon was preached by Dr. John Donne, who served as

Lincoln's Inn (New Hall and library)

preacher to Lincoln's Inn for six years before moving on to an appointment as Dean of St. Paul's Cathedral. The chapel bell has tolled curfew for Lincoln's Inn every evening at 9:00 o'clock since 1596. It has also been the custom to toll the bell whenever a "bencher" of the Inn dies. Barristers from around the grounds would then send clerks out to discover who had passed away. It was perhaps an echo of this custom that inspired Donne to write in 1624,

> No man is an island, entire of itself; every man is a piece
> of the continent, a part of the main; if a clod be washed
> away by the sea, Europe is the less, as well as if a promon-
> tory were, as well as if a manor of thy friend's or of thine
> own were; any man's death diminishes me, because I am
> involved in mankind; and therefore never send to know
> for whom the bell tolls; it tolls for thee.

*Return to the large square you have just left, through either arch, and continue to walk through the grounds, skirting the lovely garden on your right. Head for the large red brick (with striking cream trim) Victorian Tudor New Hall and Library.* These buildings are not normally open to the public, but occasionally you can get into a conversation with an Inn member who will offer to take you inside. *To the left of the New Hall is an ornate gatehouse made of the same red brick and cream stone. Walk to it and exit Lincoln's Inn via that gate. You will now find yourself on the largest square in central London—Lincoln's Inn Fields.* It was laid out formally by the Neoclassic architect and scene

41

Lincoln's Inn

designer Inigo Jones in 1618. *On the south side of the square (ahead of you and to the left) is the hall and buildings of the Royal College of Surgeons.* Most of the rest of the elegant premises surrounding the central park are occupied by law offices, but in the 17th century residents like the flamboyant actress Nell Gwynn gave the area a slightly different tone. The square was also one of London's more popular dueling grounds before it was fenced in.

*Walk around the square to your right looking for Number 13, which is the Sir John Soane's Museum.* It is open Tuesday through Saturday from 10 to 5, and admission is free, but groups must book in advance. This remarkable house contains the quirky and constantly amazing collections of the distinguished architect whose main claim to fame was the original design for the Bank of England building. The house and its furnishings were left to the nation and are displayed substantially as they were left on the day of Soane's death in 1837. Inside is a wealth of material including a fair number of interesting theatrical paintings and busts. Make sure you do not miss the little Shakespearean Recess on your way up to the second floor. There are also statuary of all periods, exquisite furniture, jewel-like rooms, Egyptian sarcophagi, and finally the stunning picture room with Hogarth's brilliant paintings of the Rake's Progress. Soane acquired the Hogarth paintings from the actor David Garrick, who originally had them in his country house along the Thames. Don't be afraid to ask questions while touring the house—the caretakers are friendly and well informed.

**Sir John Soane's
Museum**

*Upon leaving the Soane Museum continue to your right around the square toward the southwest corner where* **Portsmouth Street** *leaves Lincoln's Inn Fields.*

*As you walk down Portsmouth Street you will pass on your left a quaint little building that claimed to be Charles Dickens' original* **Old Curiosity Shop.** Most sources put the Old Curiosity Shop somewhere behind

**The Old Curiosity Shop**

the National Portrait Gallery at the bottom of Charing Cross Road, but this one is indeed old and certainly has plenty of Old English atmosphere.

*Bend to the right a bit at the Old Curiosity Shop and move down Sheffield Street until you reach **Portugal Street**.* It was at this corner that Mr. Thomas Killigrew, with a precious royal patent freshly in hand, installed a company of actors in November of 1660. The building had been remodeled from a tennis court, and was now called the Vere Street Theatre. Killigrew and his King's Men opened the theatre on December 8, 1660 with a production of Shakespeare's *Henry IV, Part I.* A bit later came a production of *Othello,* which probably featured the first appearance in an English public theatre of a native born professional actress in a major dramatic role. We do not know her name or the exact date, but she did apparently act the role of Desdemona sometime before the end of 1660.

*Turn left now into Portugal Street. It takes a quick bend left, crosses St. Clement's Lane, and then bends right past the George IV pub. Walk on for another block along the side of the British Library of Political and Economic Science until you reach Carey Street coming in from the right.* Had you been walking here in 1660 you would have seen on your left another theatre converted from a tennis court (Lisle's Tennis Court). It's also true that had you been walking here on October 10, 1940 you might have had another kind of theatrical experience during a German air raid. *Look at the shrapnel hole in the old W. H. Smith sign on the building to your right.*

But back to Lisle's Tennis Court in June of 1660. It was leased by the second Restoration patent holder, Sir William Davenant. *Davenant called his newly converted tennis court the **Lincoln's Inn Fields Theatre** and opened it in June of 1660, a full five months before Mr. Killigrew got his Vere Street theatre operating.* Davenant's first production was a revival of *The Siege of Rhodes,* an opera that had been done privately at his home, Rutland House, during the Commonwealth.

Its opening here therefore marked the first officially sanctioned public production of a play in London since the closing of the theatres by Oliver Cromwell in 1642. It also introduced changeable wing and drop continental scenery for the first time to the public London stage. Inigo Jones, the architect and designer we have mentioned previously, had brought the Italian scenic ideas to England and used them in his Court Masques in the early 1600s. Davenant's scene designer John Webb, who was a pupil of Jones, carried on the tradition.

Davenant's company played at the Lincoln's Inn Fields Theatre until 1671, when they moved to their Christopher Wren-designed Dorset Garden Theatre. The Lincoln's Inn Fields Theatre was not vacant for long. Killigrew and his company had moved from the Vere Street Theatre to their Theatre Royal in Bridges Street in 1663.

Unfortunately a fire destroyed that theatre in 1672 and they moved into the vacant Lincoln's Inn Fields site for two years until their own Wren-designed theatre, the first Drury Lane, was ready for them in 1674. After Killigrew's departure the building reverted to a tennis court again for a while before being demolished.

A new "second" Lincoln's Inn Fields theatre was built on this same site in 1695 by the playwright William Congreve. It was managed by the actor Thomas Betterton and featured as leading actresses Elizabeth Barry and Anne Bracegirdle. The inaugural production was Congreve's *Love for Love*, and King William III was in the audience. This second Lincoln's Inn Fields theatre was torn down by the theatrical entrepreneur Mr. Christopher Rich and his son, who built another theatre on the site, which opened in 1714 with James Quin as the major star. It was in this "third" Lincoln's Inn Fields Theatre, in 1726, that John Gay's *Beggar's Opera* premiered. It was so successful that the common joke at the time was that it made Gay rich and Rich gay. The third Lincoln's Inn Fields theatre was finally abandoned in 1732. By this time the Covent Garden area in the West End had been established as the new entertainment center of the city. Theatres and theatrical activity have never penetrated this section of the city again.

*After finishing your imaginative reconstructions of the Lincoln's Inn Fields Theatres, you can continue your stroll by turning right on Carey Street and following it all the way to* **Chancery Lane**. *The grey bulk of the rear of the* **Law Courts buildings** *will be on your right. At the* **Serle Street** *intersection note the statue of Sir Thomas More on the building to your left.* The building itself is one of those rather attractive little gems that you can often stumble on in the city. It is not ancient (only 1886), but its red brick and creamy Portland trim makes a finely chiseled appearance. Note also how the graceful swag design seems to soften and lighten the upper wall areas. Just beyond is one of the oldest pubs in the city, The Seven Stars, dating from 1602. About fifty yards along is Number 56, A.Woodhouse and Son, Ltd. (The Silver Mousetrap), that has a fascinating shop front dating from 1690.

*When you reach Chancery Lane you will see across the street and a bit to your right the freshly cleaned* **Public Record Office**. It was established in 1838 to gather together in one place all of the official records of England since the Norman conquest, including The Magna Carta, The Domesday Book, and the last will and testament of one William Shakespeare. Unfortunately the very size of the collection created a severe space problem and everything has now been moved to a new repository near Kew Gardens.

*Since there is little to see here now, you can turn right and walk down to Fleet Street to catch a bus or turn left and return to High Holborn and the Chancery Lane Tube station where you started. If you do choose to go back up to Chancery Lane, look out for* **Cursitor Street**. *When* *you reach it turn right and then make a left into* **Tooks Court.** Here in this dingy alley the sparkling 18th century dramatist, Richard Brinsley Sheridan, of *School For Scandal* fame, spent the last days of his life in what was known as a sponging house—a sort of halfway house for debtors that was one step removed from a real prison. *Follow Took's court around until you reach a tee intersection. Turn left on Furnival Street, which will take you out to Holborn viaduct. A left turn here will lead you back to the Chancery Lane underground station.*

**3**

# WALK FOUR

# STROLLING THE STRAND FROM TRAFALGAR SQUARE TO ALDWYCH

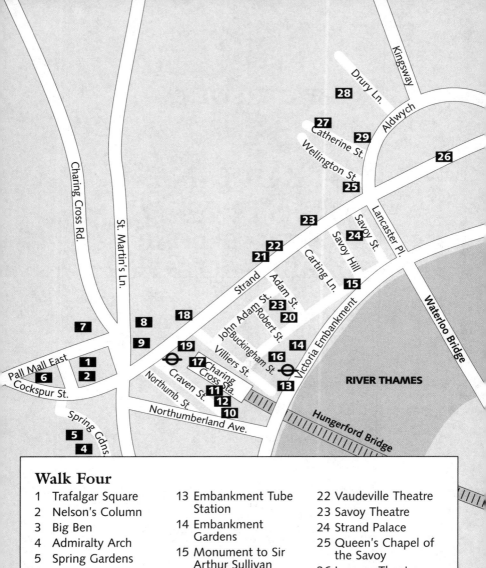

## Walk Four

1 Trafalgar Square
2 Nelson's Column
3 Big Ben
4 Admiralty Arch
5 Spring Gardens
6 Canada House
7 National Gallery
8 St. Martin-in-the-Fields
9 South Africa House
10 Playhouse
11 Charing Cross Station
12 Embankment Place

13 Embankment Tube Station
14 Embankment Gardens
15 Monument to Sir Arthur Sullivan
16 Water Gate of York House
17 Players Theatre
18 Coutts Bank
19 Charing Cross Station & Hotel
20 Adelphi
21 Adelphi Theatre

22 Vaudeville Theatre
23 Savoy Theatre
24 Strand Palace
25 Queen's Chapel of the Savoy
26 Lyceum Theatre
27 St. Mary-le-Strand
28 Duchess Theatre
29 Drury Lane Theatre
30 Strand & Aldwych Theatres
⊖ Tube Station

**STARTING POINT:** Trafalgar Square. (The nearest tube stations are Charing Cross on the Bakerloo, Northern, and Jubilee lines or Leicester Square on the Piccadilly or Northern Lines. A great many bus lines will also deposit you right on the square.)

**APPROXIMATE TIME:** One and one-half to two hours.

N *early every visitor to London will want to cover at least some parts of this route. What we have tried to do is emphasize the theatres and theatrical interest areas while mentioning briefly some of the other more general points of interest. You could do Walk Four and Five on the same day as the end of Walk Four is the beginning of Walk Five, but if that is your plan I would suggest arriving at the Trafalgar Square starting point before 10:00 AM.*

**4**

S*omeone once said, quite aptly, that* **Trafalgar Square** *is simply seven streets coming together in chaos. However you arrive, you should make your way to the center. Once stationed somewhere near the middle you can look at the fountains and the 145-foot-tall* **Nelson's column.** The spire was in place by 1842 and the huge lions were added in 1864. Edwin Landseer made the originals in clay, for casting in bronze, not helped by the fact that the aged lion, lent to him as a model by London Zoo, died before he had completed his task. As he struggled to finish the commission the artist expressed the hope that he would "neither disappoint the country nor the brave Nelson in my treatment of these symbols of our national defences."
**Whitehall** *moves down directly in front of the column to give you a distant view of the Clock Tower of the Houses of Parliament. In that tower is the 13-ton bell that is actually called* **Big Ben.**

To the right of Whitehall is **Admiralty Arch.** If you pass beneath it you will find yourself on the Mall and eventually at Buckingham Palace. That could be your route if you intend to make that grand theatrical spectacle of "Changing the Guard" a part of your London experience. The space around the arch was occupied by the Spring Gardens residential area in the 18th century and Colley Cibber (1671-1757), actor, manager, playwright, and Poet Laureate of England, lived there from 1711-1714.

49

ANNO·DECIMO·EDWARDI·SEPTIMI·REGIS·
VICTORIÆ·REGINÆ·CIVES·GRATISSIMI·MDCCCCX·

**Admiralty Arch**

*Continuing to move your eyes around the square to the right, the next major building you will see is **Canada House**, which was built by Robert Smirke in 1827.* It was originally a gentlemen's club. *The entire north side of the square, directly opposite Whitehall, is occupied by the **National Gallery**.* The main fabric of the building was designed by William Wilkins in 1838 and a major addition was completed in the early 1990s. It contains one of the truly great collections of paintings in the Western World and should be the subject of a separate visit. It's the ideal choice for that rainy day when walking just seems out of the question. During the Second World War all the pictures were removed for safety to underground storage in Wales, but at the height of the blitz Dame Myra Hess gave lunchtime piano recitals here to packed houses. Laurence Olivier and Ralph Richardson were released by the Admiralty in 1944 to lead the Old Vic Company when it returned to London, and they held their rehearsals in the National Gallery while the V2 rockets were falling all around them. Most members of the company dived for cover when the rocket-engines cut out, but these two ex-servicemen never even flinched, and carried on rehearsing.

*Turning to your right again, your eye should fall on the gleaming white spire of James Gibbs' **St. Martin-in-the-Fields** (1726).* In an older church on this same site the Restoration dramatist, George Farquhar (1678-1707), was buried. Even though he died before he was 30, he managed to produce a body of work that included two extremely fine and durable comedies, *The Recruiting Officer* (1706) and *The Beaux Stratagem* (1707). Also buried in the old St. Martin-in-the-

Fields was everybody's favorite Restoration actress, Miss Nell Gwynn (1650-1687). Nell's story has been told in any number of books as well as in the popular old melodrama, *Sweet Nell of Old Drury*. Her fame is all the more extraordinary considering she was only on stage for five years before retiring to become the mistress of Charles II.

*A bit further to the right is the newest building on the square,* **South Africa House,** *built in 1935. Our route today will take us to the right of South Africa House and up the* **Strand,** *which is a part of the major ancient route from the political center of London in Westminster to the commercial center in the City of London.* The very name of the street recalls its nearness to the river Thames in days gone by. In the middle ages the south side of the street was lined with riverside palaces of the nobility.

*Make your way now to the south or right side of the Strand, the very first intersection. This is now a wide sidewalk, which is still named* **Northumberland Street.** The Elizabethan playwright Ben Jonson (1572-1637) may have been born and did spend his boyhood on that street. *If you're already thirsty, the well known Sherlock Holmes pub is about one block down.*

*But your route today takes you to the next corner,* **Craven Street,** *where you should turn right between Boots and Next.* Benjamin Franklin lived at Number 36 on your left during his stay in London, and the commemorative plaque was restored in 1998. *At the lower end of Craven Street you pass an almost lost theatre, the* **Playhouse.** The exterior dates from 1882 and the interior dates from 1907. *It was so close to the* **Charing Cross Railroad station,** *according to Mander and Mitchenson in The Lost Theatres of London, that a part of the station collapsed into the theatre in 1905.* Alec Guinness's first professional appearance in 1934 was a non-speaking part as a juror in a play called *Libel,* which transferred to the Playhouse after opening in the Old King's Theatre in Hammersmith. He was paid £1 a week, and these humble beginnings echo those of many of the other great names encountered in these walks. This part of the city had become unfashionable by World War II, and the theatre closed down. In 1951 it became a BBC radio studio until the late seventies, and after the Corporation departed it was almost derelict for a few years, but it has now been refurbished and reopened as a theatre again.

**St. Martin-in-the-fields**

4

**The Playhouse**

*Turn left now into* **Embankment Place.** Until the late 1980s this huge arch under the Charing Cross Station tracks was a moody, urine-smelling tunnel filled with cheap fish and chip shops and a fair number of the West End's homeless population. It appeared to be in no way altered from the time when a young Charles Dickens worked nearby in a shoe blacking shop. The author's experiences and the place were described vividly in *David Copperfield.* Now the homeless have been shooed elsewhere and the new sanitized tunnel is coldly gentrified with upscale shops.

*You will emerge from under the bridge at* **Villiers Street.** *On your right is the* **Embankment tube station,** *where you can buy lovely and reasonably priced fresh flowers from a cart that has been there since at least the middle 1970s. Head across the open area and look for an entrance into the* **Embankment Gardens**—*a lovely pocket park that is always ablaze with exquisite plantings of seasonal flowers.* The park has a bandstand and on a nice day is usually packed with tourists and workers from the surrounding stores and offices. *At the far end of the park, just past the rear entrance to the Savoy Hotel, is a marvelous* **monument to Sir Arthur Sullivan** *of the Gilbert and Sullivan partnership. Note the symbolic accoutrements off to one side—a comic mask, a lute, and a libretto. Turn around now and stroll back, taking the right hand fork in the path so that the bandstand is on your left as you approach the exit.*

*Just before you leave the park glance on your right at the old* **Water Gate of York House,** *dating from 1626.* It gives you a good sense of where the riverbank was in the 17th century before the creation of the Victoria Embankment. York House was the city dwelling place of the Archbishop of York and fronted on the Strand. Sir Francis Bacon was born there in 1561 and was baptized and buried in the old St. Martin-in-the-Fields when it was really in the fields. If you have taken the earlier walks you will also remember that you have already visited the enclaves of the Bishop of Winchester in Southwark and the Bishop of Ely near Chancery Lane. Remember, it was common for the outlying bishops to have significant estates and dwellings convenient to the political and commercial center of the country.

**4**

*If you leave the park now, you should find yourself back out on* **Villiers Street.** *Turn right up Villiers Street and look on the left for a large opening labeled "The Arches—Shopping." It is right across*

Monument to Sir Arthur Sullivan

*from a pub now called The Princess of Wales, formerly known as the Prince of Wales.*

*Turn left into the Arches arcade, which again is a poor substitute for the soot-stained gloom that used to grace the station approaches, but at least this one is dark enough to convey some small bit of mood. About halfway down you will come across the* **Players Theatre,** *which is the only purveyor of traditional British Music Hall entertainment in the West End.* The theatre history buff should immediately make arrangements to see a show if possible.

**Water Gate of York House**

Music hall seems to have begun in the upper rooms of neighborhood taverns in the 18th century. It spread to larger clubs or halls such as Sadler's Wells in the 19th century after gas lighting made longer evening journeys safer and more practical. It reached the peak of its popularity in the later years of the 19th and the early years of the 20th century. In format the music hall show is a jingoistic blend of song, comic patter, dance and occasional circus-style acts, all held together by a master of ceremonies. Like American vaudeville it fell victim to those electronic upstarts—the cinema and the wireless.

Getting back to the Players Theatre itself—the original space was back down Villiers Street about 100 yards, just across from the exit to the Embankment gardens. It was destroyed when the new Charing Cross Station complex was built. Various live theatre enterprises occupied that old building from 1867 to 1903, when the theatre closed down. It was a cinema off and on over the next 35 years, was mostly derelict during the Second World War, and then reopened as the Players Theatre in 1947. Its most memorable show was the premiere production of Sandy Wilson's musical, *The Boy Friend,* which opened in 1953. The new theatre interior is a careful copy of the old one and should continue to provide you with an appropriately Victorian evening.

*Retrace your steps back out of the arch now and turn left on Villiers Street. When you reach the Strand again, you may cross the street and examine the startling home of* **Coutts Bank.** The exterior walls of this building are by the great Georgian architect, John Nash. In the 1970s the entire building was gutted and inside the old walls the new bank

**Players Theatre**

was built. During regular business hours you can enter the three-story glass frontage and take a gleaming silver escalator up to the main banking level. There you can conduct your financial affairs amidst ferns, flowers, fountains, and fishponds. In 1994 persistent reports of the sighting of a ghost in Elizabethan dress led to some historical investigations into who lived on that site in the 16th century. One was the Fourth Duke of Norfolk, who rashly attempted to marry secretly Mary Queen of Scots, for which Queen Elizabeth I had him tried for treason and beheaded in the Tower of London in 1572. His troubled spirit was exorcised in a Roman Catholic ceremony attended by members of the present Duke of Norfolk's family, and it seems was laid to rest, as there have been no further sightings of his ghost.

The bank itself, which has occupied several sites on both sides of the Strand since 1692, has had several theatrical connections. George Campbell, an early partner, was an investor in Rich's Covent Garden in the 1730s. Several 18th century theatrical figures banked with Coutts including John Philip Kemble, Edmund Kean, and Madame Vestris. Thomas Coutts, head of the bank in the 19th century, held permanent boxes at most of the major West End theatres. He lent money to Augustus Harris, the manager of Covent Garden, and was given in gratitude a sterling silver free pass disk good for 83 years. Other important 19th century bank customers from the world of the theatre were Sir Henry Irving, the great actor-manager of the Lyceum Theatre at the other end of the Strand, the actor Charles Kean, and the manager-impresario Richard D'Oyly Carte, who produced the Gilbert and Sullivan operettas and built the Savoy theatre and the Savoy Hotel. The theatrical associations continue to this day, with Sir John Gielgud and Sir Andrew Lloyd Webber numbered among their present customers.

*Back down at the street level notice the large tree growing in the lower lobby. It does not lean toward the light because it is planted in a huge slowly rotating drum.*

*Outside again you are in a position to take note across the way of the old frontage of **Charing Cross Station and Hotel**. In the open space in front of the building is the Victorian monument by E.M. Barry that commemorates the last of the twelve Eleanor crosses that were built by Edward I in the 13th century.* Eleanor of Castile, Edward's wife, died near Lincoln in 1290 while accompanying her husband on a campaign. Her body was carried back to

**E. M. Barry Victorian Monument**

Westminster and Edward erected a cross at each place where the bearers rested on the journey back to London. The original London Cross, destroyed by Cromwell's forces in 1647, actually stood at the top of Whitehall where the equestrian statue of Charles I stands today.

*Recross the Strand now back to the station side of the street and turn to your left. Watch as you walk for a tiny passage called Buckingham Arcade (just past McDonalds), which when taken through to the right, will lead to Buckingham Street and several fine original 17th-century houses.* An extraordinary number of famous men visited or lodged on this short street, but for our purposes the man of most interest was the great diarist Samuel Pepys, who lived at both Number 12 and Number 14 during the years 1679 to 1700. (The brown plaque resides on number 14 on your right.) His diaries give us some of our most revealing accounts of 17th-century theatrical and social life. *At the bottom of Buckingham Street there is a nice view of the back side of the York House Water Gate and the Embankment Gardens.*

*Retrace your steps now back up Buckingham Street and take the first turn to the right, which is John Adam Street. You are now in the area known as the Adelphi.* It is a Greek word for brothers and was chosen by the Scottish architects and developers Robert, James, and William Adam as the name for their residential and commercial development on the site beginning in 1768. A lot of the current building in the area is from the 1930s and later, but much of it still sits on the gigantic foundation arches designed by the Adam brothers to level off and use the riverbank.

*As you pass up John Adam Street, a modern apartment block now stands on the right about where number 17-19 used to be. The actor, playwright, Shakespeare scholar, and friend of George Bernard Shaw Mr. Harley Granville Barker (1877-1946) lived in a house on this site as did the modern actor Sir Cedric Hardwicke.*

*At Number 16 on the left is a blue plaque marking the site of the home, from 1803 to his death in 1827, of the caricaturist Thomas Rowlandson.* His work included some fascinating scenes of 18th century theatrical life.

*When you reach Robert Street, pause for a moment and look to your left.* This is now an office block called the Little Adelphi, but the historic Little Theatre occupied the site from 1910 until the late 1940s. The Little Theatre was a tiny bandbox of a place with 250 seats and an Adam-inspired interior. It was built on the site of the very first Coutts Bank building and had the most secure dressing rooms of any theatre in the world, since they were constructed inside the old bank's strongrooms.

The original leaseholder was the well known actress, feminist, and suffragette, Gertrude Kingston (1866-1937). Her first offering was, most aptly *Lysistrata,* and Miss Kingston apparently played the leading role for all it was worth. So that female authors could be produced without prejudice, she had the unusual policy of withholding the playwright's name from the public until after the first reviews appeared. According to Mander and Mitchenson in *The Lost Theatres of London,* George Bernard Shaw's *Fanny's First Play* was given its original production at the Little Theatre in 1911 and directed by Shaw himself. Even though the author's name was listed as Xxxxxxx Xxxx, it was so successful that it was moved to another house, where it continued to run on for a total of 622 performances, making it Shaw's longest original run. Shaw knew Gertrude Kingston well and wrote the part of Catherine II in *Great Catherine* for her. Another 1911 event was Noel Coward's first stage appearance as Prince Mussel in a children's fairy tale called *The Goldfish.*

**4**

Although a balcony was added in 1912 to expand the seating capacity, the original Adam gold and wedgwood blue auditorium was kept intact. The theatre was damaged during a German air raid during World War I, rebuilt, and then severely damaged again by bombing in World War II. Even the safest air raid shelters of any theatre in London (the old Coutts bank vaults again), could not save the Little Theatre. After standing derelict for more than four years after the Second World War, the building was finally demolished and replaced by an office block.

*Turn to your right now, away from the Little Theatre site, and walk up **Robert Street**. On your left, at Number 8, you will pass the Royal Society for the encouragement of Arts, Manufactures and Commerce. On your right (note blue plaque) was the Adelphi Court, an apartment and hotel complex, where several literary figures lived at one time or another. At Number 1 young Master William Betty lived from 1833-1845.* As a child of ten, Betty played major tragic roles like Hamlet and Macbeth, made a small fortune, and retired to live a life of ease. Sir James Barrie, author of *Peter Pan* and *The Admirable Crichton*; and John Galsworthy, author of a series of realistic social problem plays such as *Strife* (1909) and *Justice* (1910), were both tenants in this block. *When you reach the end of the street turn left and cross in front of the Art Deco New Adelphi,* which was built after the grand Adam terrace of that same name was demolished in 1936. Stop at a convenient place about half way down the length of the building and read the following:

LONDON COUNTY COUNCIL
ROBERT ADAM
THOMAS HOOD
JOHN GALSWORTHY
SIR JAMES BARRIE
AND
OTHER EMINENT ARTISTS
AND WRITERS LIVED HERE

From the 1770s the original Adelphi was one of London's smartest addresses and it attracted a bevy of glittering names. One of the very first and most distinguished of the old Adelphi residents was the 18th century actor/manager David Garrick. He moved into the center apartment facing the river in 1772 and lived there until his death in 1779. The cream of the world of arts and letters passed through his drawing room including Dr. Samuel Johnson, Sir Joshua Reynolds, Robert Adam, Dr. Charles Burney, and Fanny Burney his vivacious daughter. Mrs. Garrick lived on after her husband's death for another forty-three years and died in the front drawing room that looked out over the Thames.

**4**

Other theatrical residents of the old Adelphi were Richard D'Oyly Carte who lived in apartment number 4 from 1888-1901 while he was producing the Savoy Operas; and George Bernard Shaw, who occupied apartment number 10 from 1900 to 1919. The Adam brothers themselves kept apartment number 4, right next to Garrick's for several years. The occupant of number 9 in 1775 was a Mr. John Robinson, Secretary of the Treasury. His rather vague theatre connection occurs as a result of the acid tongue of dramatist Richard Brinsley Sheridan. It seems that Robinson had been given the task of disseminating ministerial bribes from his treasury position. Sheridan got wind of it and attacked the government's corruption in Parliament. When challenged to name the wrongdoer, Sheridan gazed at the Treasury Bench and replied, "Yes, I could name him as soon as I can say Jack Robinson." And we remember old Jack to this day.

*Finish your cross in front of the length of the 1936 Adelphi Terrace now. Turn the corner at the end of the building and you will be on Adam Street.* The brothers were definitely not given to modesty when it came to naming streets. *Keep your eye out on the right for Number 7 Adam Street with its dark brick and cream trim.* It is a virtually unspoiled Adam house and gives you a superb sense of the distinctive Adam decorative style. *Number 9 became the new home of the Green Room Club in 1997.* The original club was

**Adam house**

founded by David Garrick, and it has traditionally catered for the more proletarian end of the acting profession, rather than for the distinguished leading actors who frequent the club actually named after Garrick. The Green Room Club has been forced to be much more peripatetic in its premises; its most recent previous home was opposite the Stage Door of the Haymarket Theatre. Otherwise the solid blocks of newer buildings today even cover up old streets such as the now vanished Salisbury Street where Oscar Wilde once lived. Cecil Street was also once

**Green Room Club**

**4**

located somewhere to your right. The actor Edmund Kean (1790-1833) lived there while a young unknown. The story is told how after his first big success he ran up the stairs at number 21 Cecil street and shouted to his wife and son, "Mary! You shall ride in your carriage, and Charley shall go to Eton."

*You have now almost circumnavigated the new Adelphi Terrace with its sleek 1930-style streamlining. Continue ahead on Adam Street until you return to the Strand. You will be passing on your left the site of another one of those lost theatres so lovingly described by Mander and Mitchenson. This time it is the Tivoli Theatre of Varieties, which was built in 1890 on the site of a beer garden and restaurant at the corner of Adam Street and the Strand.* It operated as a music hall until 1914, then stood derelict for awhile, and was finally demolished. The Tivoli Cinema was built on the site in 1923, but it was damaged during the Blitz and it too was pulled down to make way for a department store and finally the current New South Wales House.

*Back out on the Strand proper you can see, directly across the busy street, the facade of a surviving theatre: **The Adelphi.*** This is the fourth theatre on the site since 1806. The current Adelphi seats over 1400

people and opened in 1930 with the Rodgers and Hart musical, *Evergreen*. There is little of real historical import to note about the shows that filled the theatre up to the late 1950s. Then Bea Lillie opened *Auntie Mame*. That success was followed by the scenically spectacular production of Lionel Bart's *Blitz* in 1962. Anna Neagle played herself in a musical called *Charlie Girl* beginning in 1965 and it ran for almost 2000 performances—until 1971. In recent years the theatre has seen a string of mostly long-running musicals, including Andrew Lloyd Webber's *Sunset Boulevard*.

The Adelphi has the melancholy distinction of being the only theatre in the country where an actor was assassinated at the stage door. This was William Terriss, a leading member of Henry Irving's company for some years, who was stabbed in the back in 1897 by a crazed small-part actor with an imagined grievance. More than 50,000 Londoners lined the streets for Terriss's funeral, though Irving prophesied gloomily, and accurately, that nobody would be hanged for murdering an actor. Terriss was known affectionately to the British public as "Breezy Bill," and also as "No. 1, Adelphi Terriss," since much of his best work was done at this address. On the centenary of his death Sir Donald Sinden unveiled a plaque commemorating the event.

*Not too far to the right of the Adelphi, you will also see the front of the* **Vaudeville Theatre.** This is the third theatre built on that site since 1870, although the frontage now visible was retained from the second rebuilding in 1891. The interior has seen some major redecoration since the 1926 rebuilding but no real structural changes. Its fare has been mainly light comedy and musical revue. The longest run in the house was the musical *Salad Days,* which carried on for over 2300 performances from 1954 to 1960.

*You should still be standing at the intersection of The Strand and John Adam Street. Turn right and continue your walk down the Strand. At the corner of* **Carting Lane** *is the Coal Hole tavern.* In the early 19th century it was frequented by the coal heavers who unloaded barges on the Thames. The actor Edmund Kean, who as we just noted, lived nearby, frequented this tavern and according to John Wittich founded a club there for "repressed husbands who were not allowed to sing in their baths."

*Moving on another few steps will bring you to the head of Savoy Court, the only two-way street in London where you drive on the right. To learn about the Savoy, cross the court and read the series of metal plaques that are*

**Vaudeville Theatre**

**Savoy Court**

*mounted along the side of the building. When you finish the story you will be almost at the entrance of the luxurious, world famous Savoy Hotel. To your right will be the equally famous **Savoy Theatre**.* Richard D'Oyly Carte built the first Savoy Theatre in 1881 and looked convincingly to the future by making it the first theatre in London to be lit by incandescent light. His remarks at the opening, as cited by Mander and Mitchenson, did show, however, that he regarded the experiment with some fear and trepidation. In lines that are amusing today, D'Oyly Carte assured his patrons that the entire building had also been piped for gas and that the pilot light on the central chandelier would always be kept lit so that if the new lights failed, the whole interior could be illuminated within seconds by reliable gas mantles.

The Savoy Theatre opened on October 10, 1881, with Gilbert and Sullivan's *Patience*. The Prince and Princess of Wales were in the audience. From then on until 1907, it saw a set of now classic pearls with softly glowing names like *Iolanthe, The Sorcerer, The Mikado,* and *The Gondoliers,* and, apart from what became known generally as the Savoy Operas, it also had a success with *Merrie England.* It then fell on hard times and was closed for a while, until in 1907 the Vedrenne/Granville Barker partnership had a run of successful Shaw revivals. Most spectacularly, Harvey Granville Barker between 1912-14 put on seasons of *The Winter's Tale, Twelfth Night,* and *A Midsummer Night's Dream,* which revolutionized the presentation of Shakespeare. In the 1920s there were several long-run hits culminating with R.C. Sherriff's highly charged war drama *Journey's End* in 1929. The story of this show could occupy a book by itself. It had originally been scheduled for a two-performance trial run at the Apollo Theatre. A struggling young actor by the name of Laurence Olivier took on the role of Capt. Dennis Stanhope for the princely sum of five pounds. The short run was impressive enough for the producers to book the Savoy Theatre and try a regular run. Olivier, however, had another offer to play a leading role in a production of *Beau Geste* at a guaranteed thirty pounds a week and dropped out of the cast. The role was recast with a young man name named Colin Clive. Needless to say, *Journey's End* opened to acclaim, ran for over 600 performances and made a momentary star of the young man who took Olivier's place. *Beau Geste* ran only four weeks and the future Sir Laurence would have to wait a bit longer for fame and fortune.

When *Journey's End* closed, the theatre was completely rebuilt in the smooth, sleek, 1930 streamlined style that you see on the frontage today. Throughout the next two decades the Savoy was primarily the home of comedies with occasional light opera seasons thrown in for good measure. Tom Conti changed this frivolous image in 1978 when he opened in Brian Clark's stimulating and controversial *Whose Life Is It Anyway*. It was back to light hearted fun in 1982 when the farce of the decade, Michael Frayn's *Noises Off* opened its four-year run. Tragedy struck in 1991 when a disastrous fire destroyed the entire theatre. *Look for some pictures of the damage at the Theatre Museum.* The building and its decor were faithfully restored and it reopened on July 19, 1993. One new twist is that the Savoy Hotel swimming pool is now located on top of the reconstructed theatre. One wonders if provision has been made to simply pull a drain plug if there is another blaze.

While we are here we might mention that D'Oyly Carte also built the Savoy Hotel in 1903. This elegant hostelry was constructed with a bathroom and lavatory for each room, which was an unheard of extravagance at the turn of the century. Cesar Ritz was the first manager and the famed Escoffier was an early chef. The first martini is said to have been mixed in its American Bar, and of course you may still dine in the Thameside Restaurant where the Peach Melba was created in honor of the famed singer Nellie Melba. It remains today one of the finest hotels in London and the preferred stopping and dining place for the stars of international business, politics, and entertainment.

*Return now to the Strand and take a right turn to continue your stroll. Across the street another hotel should catch your eye. Not quite the Savoy, but elegant still, the* **Strand Palace** *stands on the site of Exeter Hall, a 19th century meeting and recital hall that once was graced by the likes of the inimitable Jenny Lind, "the Swedish Nightingale."* Note on your right the venerable restaurant Simpsons, where the traditional English dinner of Roast Beef and Yorkshire Pudding is king.

*At the street sign for Savoy Buildings is another Edmund Kean association. According to the wall plaque, this was the site of the Fountain Tavern wherein met the Fountain Club, and also the Wolf Club, of which Kean was a leading member.*

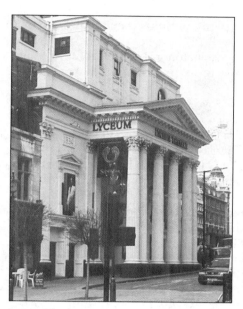

**Lyceum Theatre**

At Savoy Street Gilbert and Sullivan fans might wish to take a side trip. Turn right to find the **Queen's Chapel of the Savoy**, built in 1501, and the only surviving part of the ancient Savoy Palace. There is a stained glass window in the church dedicated to Richard D'Oyly Carte. Members of the public are welcome to attend the 11 AM service on Sundays and some on weekdays. Check the noticeboard outside.

Otherwise, continue your stroll in the Strand for one more short block to the busy intersection of **Lancaster Place** where traffic is fed over the **Waterloo Bridge.**

Cross this congested artery. If you look back slightly across the Strand to the north up **Wellington Street,** you will see the classical portico of the once great **Lyceum Theatre.** The first Lyceum opened in 1772 and actually faced out into the Strand. It hosted exhibitions, concerts, and assorted entertainments including the first waxwork shop of Madame Tussaud. Strangely, its survival seems to have been built on the one major enemy of historic theatres—fire. From its inception the Lyceum had no licence to perform plays, which accounts for its potpourri programing. But in 1809, when the Theatre Royal Drury Lane burned down, the Lyceum owner got a performance licence to receive the Drury Lane's homeless company. He also managed to retain the licence on a periodic basis after the Drury Lane company moved back to their new premises.

In 1830 fire caught up to the Lyceum itself and ultimately a new building was constructed slightly west of the old and this time fronting on Wellington Street. This second theatre hung on for several years, but by 1855 it was bankrupt. Once again a fire saved the day. The Covent Garden theatre burned in 1856 and the company was moved to the Lyceum for two years.

From here it was not long until the arrival of Henry Irving, who became the chief actor and manager of the theatre in 1878. With his leading lady Ellen Terry, he gave Londoners a distinguished series of productions for the next twenty four years. His long and enterprising tenure at the Lyceum is generally acknowledged as one of the major reasons for the rise in status and respectability of the acting profession in the minds of the British public. In 1896, Mr. Irving appeared on Queen Victoria's yearly Honors List and thereby became Sir Henry Irving, the first ever of his profession to be knighted in Great Britain.

The theatre itself did not survive Irving's departure by much and was razed, except for the portico and rear wall, in 1904. Rebuilt as a music hall, it has had a checkered career since, and was almost demolished on several occasions. The last actor to tread its boards before the outbreak of World War II was John Gielgud, whose Hamlet then went on to appear at Kronborg Castle in Elsinore itself, as the war-clouds gathered. The Lyceum stood derelict for much of the war, and was then adapted for use as a dance hall and as a site for rock concerts. In 1985 the National Theatre's successful re-staging of *The Mysteries* there created new interest in its survival, and after a major rebuilding and redecoration the Lyceum reopened in 1996 with a revival of *Jesus Christ Superstar,* not perhaps the closest show to the Irving tradition, but at least it is now a theatre again.

*Look now past Number 346 Strand, rebuilt as a new hotel, to the little island created between the curve of **Aldwych** and the Strand, dominated now by the facade of Citibank. You are gazing at the site of another famous lost theatre—the (second) Gaiety. From 1903 to 1939 it was one of the stellar showplaces of the city.* When it opened in 1903, Edward VII and Queen Alexandra were in attendance. As another sidelight, one of the offices in the Gaiety building housed the Wireless Telegraph Company of one Mr. Marconi, who operated a station and studio there until 1922 when it became the British Broadcasting Company. *Another piece of the past that doesn't have to be imagined is visible just ahead down the Strand. The church of **St. Mary-le-Strand** was built by the same James Gibbs who designed St. Martin-in-the-Fields in 1714.*

*Bring yourself back to the present now and let your eyes wander up the gentle curve of Aldwych.* You are looking at one of the major urban re-development projects of turn of the century London. In order to get a better route from the West End to the river and to widen the Strand, the crescent ahead of you and the broad expanse of Kingsway at the top of the crescent were literally carved out of 30 acres of densely populated urban real estate. Some of the leveled land was unmistakably filled with slums, but several commercial properties, including some legitimate theatres, were also destroyed.

*Cross the Strand now, and start up the left hand side of the Aldwych crescent. At **Catherine Street** on the left you can look up toward the tiny Duchess Theatre (747 seats), which dates from 1929.* Two of Emlyn Williams' best plays opened here and ran for over a year each. They were *Night Must Fall* (1935) and *The Corn is Green* (1938). T.S. Eliot's *Murder in the Cathedral* had its first West End production here in 1936 and Noel Coward's *Blithe Spirit* had already run a year at the

Piccadilly Theatre before it transferred to the Duchess in 1942, where it continued through 1945 running up a total of 1997 performances.

In 1974 the nude revue *Oh Calcutta!* transferred into the theatre and for the next four years the house was filled with high class bodies and low class jokes. The Duchess also holds the West End record for shortest run ever. *The Intimate Review*, which premiered in 1930, did not even survive its opening night. The curtain was dropped and the audience dismissed before the conclusion of the show.

A bit farther on up Catherine Street was the site of the first Gaiety Theatre, whose name became the watchword for burlesque and musical comedy from 1864 to its close in 1903. The first Gaiety was one of the theatres that was destroyed in order to create the Aldwych and Kingsway. In those days elegant young ladies received the night's program engraved on a perfumed fan and the chorus girls of impresario George Edwards were as famous in London society as they were in theatre. The "Gaiety Girls" were a vibrant symbol of the gay nineties in London.

*As you stand here you will also be able to see at the top of the street the facade of London's oldest and arguably second most famous theatre after Shakespeare's Globe, the Drury Lane (1812).* We will deal with its fascinating history during the Covent Garden walk.

*Directly across Catherine Street from you is the* **Strand Theatre** *(1905). It has an identical exterior to its partner on the other side of the Waldorf Hotel,* **The Aldwych.** The Strand has not known a good deal of important activity, although the great Italian actress Eleonora Duse did perform there with her company in the inaugural season of 1905. The major long runs have been light comedies such as *Arsenic and Old Lace,* which ran for 1337 performances beginning in 1942, and a rather mild comedy with a saucily provocative title, *No Sex Please We're British.* This show opened at the Strand in 1971 and was shifted to the Garrick Theatre in the 1980s where it continued to play building up a run of over 5000 performances. When it closed it was billed as the world's longest running comedy and the second

**Strand Theatre**

longest running play in the West End. *The Mousetrap* at forty-plus years and still going should have no trouble staying in first place.

*To get back to business, Ivor Novello (1893-1951), lived in an apartment above the Strand Theatre for many years. There's a blue plaque above the door of #11.* Novello, like Noel Coward, was an actor, playwright, composer, lyricist, and producer. He wrote more than twenty plays, most of them comedies or musical reviews, and starred in a vast majority of them as well. Unlike Noel Coward, Novello never did become a major celebrity in the United States. He is remembered, however, as the composer of one of World War I's most popular songs, "Keep the Home Fires Burning."

**4**

*Walk on now past the Waldorf Hotel to the **Aldwych Theatre**, which was for several years the London home of the Royal Shakespeare Company.* The RSC now resides at the Barbican for six months each year. Like its companion theatre, The Strand, the Aldwych has American associations. The brothers Shubert were the original lease holders of the Strand and the Aldwych was built by a partnership that included Mr. Charles Frohman, another financial giant in the 19th century American theatre.

In the 1920s the Aldwych was most famous for a series of productions now known as the Aldwych farces. Many of them were by Mr. Ben Travers, whose name was given new life by a successful revival of *Plunder* (1928) at the Royal National Theatre a few years back.

To recount the successes at the theatre just during the RSC tenure would take a book itself, but two modern events do bear noting. From 1964 to 1973 Mr. Peter Daubeny and the RSC presented what was known as The World Theatre Season at the theatre. They brought the best theatre companies of the world to London to perform in their native languages. Thus this house has not only seen the best that the Royal Shakespeare Company has to offer, but it has also seen companies from most of Western Europe, the United States, Africa, Eastern Europe, Canada, and the Far East. The Aldwych was also home to the RSC's original eight-hour production of *Nicholas Nickleby* in 1980. In recent years it has housed transfers from theatres ranging in size from the Almeida to the National, as well as productions by West End commercial managements.

*Continue your stroll along the crescent toward the broad expanse of **Kingsway**, which you will reach shortly. On your right, dominating the end of Kingsway is the vast building known as Bush House, which contains the offices and studios of the BBC's World Service.*

*You are now at the ending point for this walk. Public transportation is available by turning left on Kingsway and walking up to the Holborn Tube Station. There are also plenty of buses running on the Strand that will take you back to Trafalgar Square or Piccadilly.*

*Should you still have shoe leather and stamina left, you could turn immediately to Walk Five and continue on toward St. Paul's Cathedral.*

# WALK FIVE

❀

# A FLEET RAMBLE TO ST. PAUL'S:
## FROM TEMPLE BAR TO THE CATHEDRAL

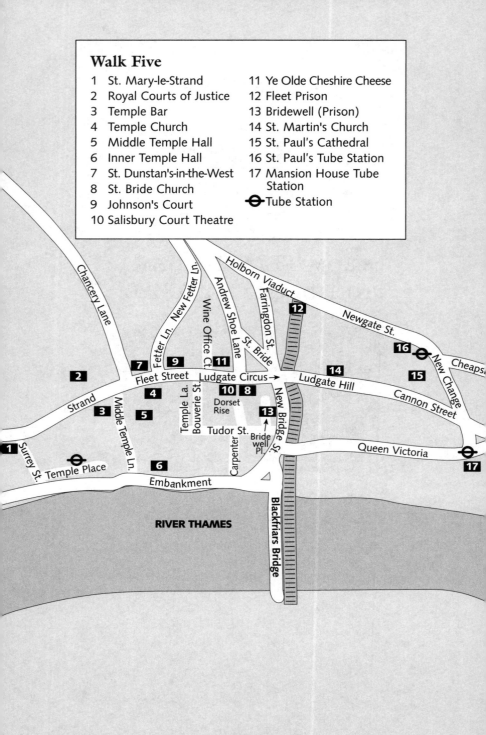

## Walk Five

1  St. Mary-le-Strand
2  Royal Courts of Justice
3  Temple Bar
4  Temple Church
5  Middle Temple Hall
6  Inner Temple Hall
7  St. Dunstan's-in-the-West
8  St. Bride Church
9  Johnson's Court
10 Salisbury Court Theatre
11 Ye Olde Cheshire Cheese
12 Fleet Prison
13 Bridewell (Prison)
14 St. Martin's Church
15 St. Paul's Cathedral
16 St. Paul's Tube Station
17 Mansion House Tube Station

⊖ Tube Station

Chancery Lane
Fetter Ln.
New Fetter Ln.
Holborn Viaduct
Wine Office Ct.
Andrew Shoe Lane
St. Bride
Farringdon St.
Newgate St.
Cheaps.
New Change

**7**  **9**  **11**  **12**  **16** ⊖  **15**

**2**  Fleet Street  Ludgate Circus →  Ludgate Hill  **14**

Strand  **4**  Temple La.  Bouverie St.  **10**  **8**  **13**  Cannon Street

**3**  Middle Temple Ln.  **5**  Dorset Rise  New Bridge St.

Tudor St.  Bride well Pl.

**1**  Surrey St.  Temple Place  **6**  Carpenter  Queen Victoria  **17**

Embankment

Blackfriars Bridge

**RIVER THAMES**

Thiis is essentially a continuation of Walk Four, and in it you will visit the Middle and Inner Temple, Fleet Street, Dr. Johnson's house, The Cheshire Cheese, St. Bride's Church, the sites of some long forgotten theatres, and St. Paul's Cathedral. (Middle and Inner Temple, like the other Inns of Court, are closed on weekends.)

**5**

*From Temple Station, make your way left out of the exit on Temple Place, past the river frontage of the Howard Hotel, and then turn right on Surrey Street and proceed up to the Strand where you will turn right.* William Congreve, the playwright (1670-1729), lived on Surrey Street for some years. Nearby was the home of Anne Bracegirdle (1663-1749), the actress who was an extremely close friend of his.

*You should be able to see ahead of you a sort of traffic island in the middle of the street on which the Wren church of St. Clement Dane's (1682) is perched.* The famous bells that rang out "Oranges and Lemons" were destroyed during a World War II bombing. The dramatist Thomas Otway (1652-85), whose most famous play was *Venice Preserved* in 1682, was buried in an older church on the site. Mrs. Sarah Siddons, the pre-eminent 18th century tragic actress, had lodgings somewhere nearby as well. *Back up the Strand and behind you is the graceful and delicate church of St. Mary-le-Strand (1717) designed by James Gibbs.* We mentioned it briefly in Walk Four. You may wish to compare it to St. Martin-in-the-Fields. Since Gibbs also did the steeple on St. Clement Danes in 1719, we have three of his spires in a row as we move down the

**St. Clement Dane's**

**St. Mary-le-Strand**

**5**

**Royal Courts of Justice**

Strand. *Pass St. Clement Danes on either side. Pause and enter if you wish.* This is now the official Royal Air Force Church, so behind the large and imposing statue of the great Victorian statesman, W.E. Gladstone, you will see those of the wartime RAF Chiefs, Fighter Command's Lord Dowding, and Bomber Command's Sir Arthur Harris.

   *Coming up shortly on your left you will see the grounds of the **Royal Courts of Justice** where civil court cases are tried.* Courtrooms are open to the public and you can check for details on visiting at the main

Twinings;
Wig &
Pen Club

entrance if you wish. *You will also want to cast your eyes on the rather agreeable frontages along your right. There is a lovely narrow old pub called the George and just a few steps beyond #216, the site of Twinings original tea salesroom dating from 1706. #230 is the Wig and Pen Club.*

*About 100 yards ahead, a stone plinth surmounted by a strange beast known as a griffin will catch your eye. This is the site of* **Temple Bar,** *a former gate into the City of London.* To this day, when the Sovereign wishes to visit the City of London, she pauses at this boundary and requests permission of the Lord Mayor to enter. Inside the boundaries of the City of London the Lord Mayor ranks ahead of even the Queen's own family in terms of protocol. *It is also at this point that the Strand becomes* **Fleet Street,** *taking its name from the now covered Fleet River that runs into the Thames at the bottom of the hill ahead of you.*

*At number 1 Fleet Street just inside Temple Bar and to your right is the office of Child's Bank, England's oldest private bank (1671).* Pretty Nell Gwynn, the actress and mis-

**5**

**Child's Bank**

**Gatehouse into Middle Temple Lane**

tress of Charles II, was a customer of Child's, as were Samuel Pepys, John Dryden, Oliver Cromwell, Horace Walpole, and indeed even royalty, including Charles II, James II, and William III. At an earlier time this was also the site of The Devil Tavern, where Ben Jonson met with his "Apollo Club" cronies to eat, drink, and jest.

*Just a few more steps and on your right you will find the 1684 Christopher Wren gatehouse into* **Middle Temple Lane.** *Enter it. Once through this gate you are in the precincts of The Middle Temple.* There are four so called Inns of Court in London (Lincoln's Inn, Gray's Inn, Middle Temple, Inner Temple). The Inns have the exclusive prerogative to call persons to the Bar. They provide lecturers and examinations for students and office space for barristers. In earlier years they also provide lodging for members and other private citizens. If you have ever watched *Rumpole of the Bailey,* you may see some familiar sights. Rumpole's firm has offices here and some of the exteriors have been filmed in and around the Middle and Inner Temple.

*On your right, shortly after entering Brick Court, Oliver Goldsmith (1730-74) lived out the last nine years of his life.* The actual building is now demolished. We will visit his grave outside the Temple Church shortly. *Continuing down Middle Temple Lane, the next open space on the right is the Fountain Court. The dominant building on the court is* **Middle Temple Hall,** *which used to be open to visitors, but now appears to be permanently closed.* The hall, built originally in 1570 and restored after heavy bomb damage in World War II, has one of the finest double hammerbeam roofs in all of England. Its theatrical interest comes from a February 2, 1602 diary

entry by John Manningham, a barrister of the Temple. Manningham saw a play in the hall called *Twelfth Night* and a character called Malvolio caught his particular fancy.

Manningham's diary is also the source of the only contemporary anecdote about Shakespeare. He reports a story that a young lady was so taken by Richard Burbage's performance in *Richard III* that she invited him to come to her chambers in costume after the performance. Shakespeare apparently overheard the plan, went on ahead, and was himself being entertained when came a knock at the door and the announcement that Richard III was at hand, whereupon Shakespeare sent down the message: "William the Conqueror was before Richard III."

*Stroll into the interior of the court toward the ancient fountain (1681) where Ruth Pinch met her brother Tom in Dickens' **Martin Chuzzlewit**. At the rear of the court turn left down the stairs into Garden Court.*

*From here you can look out to your left over the Middle Temple Garden and believe if you will the legend that this was the very garden where Richard Plantagenet (who becomes the Duke of York) and the Earl of Somerset quarreled and ordered their supporters to show their loyalties by plucking a red rose or a white rose.* There is no hard evidence suggesting that the War of the Roses actually did begin here, but in Shakespeare's *Henry VI, Part 1*, Act II, scene 4, Plantagenet leaves with a group of four to eat dinner. This was the traditional number in a "mess" at the Middle Temple Hall.

*Since the garden is not open to the public, you must retrace your steps back to Middle Temple Lane. Look but do not turn to your right. If you went that way you would soon pass by the former residence of poet and playwright William Butler Yeats and Crown Office Row where the critic and author Charles Lamb was born. But our route today takes us back to the left. Cross over the lane and move back up toward Fleet Street looking out on the right for a small passage leading to the Pump Court.* Henry Fielding (1707-54), novelist and playwright (*Tom Thumb*) rented

**Brick Court fountain**

**Inner Temple Hall**

chambers in this court. Fielding's prime reputation today rests on his novels, but in his early years he had a significant influence on the London theatre scene. His satirical plays were among the main reasons for the passage of the Licensing Act of 1737.

*Walk on through Pump Court and out through the cloisters at the other end. You are now in another court and on your right is the **Inner Temple Hall**.* The ancient hall on the site (the current one is a reconstruction of a 19th century building) saw the production of many plays in the 16th and 17th centuries. Thomas Norton and William Sackville were both members of the Inner Temple when their play *Gorboduc*, the first English tragedy in blank verse, was produced in the Inner Temple Hall in 1561. The records indicate that Queen Elizabeth I was in attendance.

*To your left is a true architectural treasure. **The Temple Church**, dating from 1185, is one of five surviving round churches in England.* It is usually open and a closer inspection is called for. In the older circular portion there are some fine recumbent effigies of 12th and 13th century knights. On the interior walls, just above head height, is a series of carved faces. Some are calm and beatific, but others are fanciful or grotesque. The only theatrical figure buried in the church is John Marston (1575-1634) a minor Elizabethan dramatist and satirist.

*Leave the church and turn right, circling the rounded end of the building. You will pass the great west doors (now sealed) and be moving up Inner Temple Lane. Make a right turn at the first opening labeled Goldsmith Building and move down the walk parallel to the north side of the church.* Next to the statue of a long forgotten magistrate named

**Temple Church**

Johannes Hiccocks is a slightly raised slab with the barely legible sentence, "Here Lies Oliver Goldsmith." Goldsmith, like Fielding and Swift, is perhaps best known as a novelist today, but his *She Stoops To Conquer* (1773) remains one of the true classics and most often produced of all 18th century British dramas.

*Return to Inner Temple Lane, turn right, and head back toward Fleet Street, exiting beneath Prince Henry's room. If you look back above your head after you re-enter Fleet Street you will see one of the few pieces of original half-timber work left in London. It dates from 1610 and you may visit one of the rooms associated with Henry, the elder son of James I, between 11 and 2, Monday through Saturday. Admission is free. The stairs are to the left of the archway.*

**Grave of Oliver Goldsmith**

*Continuing once again down Fleet Street you will note across the way the interesting octagonal church of* **St. Dunstan's-in-the-West** *(1832). Make your way across the street to examine it more closely.* The figure of Queen Elizabeth I over the east vestry porch was taken from the old Lud Gate into the City of London. Two figures associated with the Elizabethan theatre, Philip Massinger and Thomas Campion, were buried in an older church on the site. Massinger's best known work is a play titled *A New Way To Pay Old Debts,* which was written in 1625. One of its leading roles, Sir Giles Overreach, was a particular favorite of actor Edmund Kean. It was frequently in the 19th century repertoire, but has fallen out of favour in the 20th; the last great exponent was Donald Wolfit in his post-war tours. Campion was a poet and court masque composer who touched the theatre briefly via his friendship with Philip Rosseter, who directed a company of boy actors at the Whitefriars Theatre not too far from here. The clock (1761) is also worth a look as you pass by.

*Continue on down the street past* **Fetter Lane** *into what used to be the very heart of British Pressland.* The call of the open spaces and cheaper rentals of Docklands has denuded the area of newspaper publishers, but the streets seem no less busy now. It's only the character that has changed.

*Keep your eyes ahead as you move around a slight bend in the street and you will see ahead of you a famous view of* **St. Paul's Cathedral** *with the small slender spire of St. Martin's Without Ludgate in front of it and acting as a foil for the massive dome.*

*Right about at this point (#167) you should also find on your left* **Johnson's Court,** *which will lead you through a number of intriguing twists and turns to Gough Square and the nicely preserved 18th century home of Dr. Samuel Johnson, where you can see a statue of his cat, Hodge.* Although Johnson did not have a great fondness for actors, he did know many of them. The house has several nice theatrical prints and an old chest that David Garrick used for costume storage. *It is open from 11 to 5, except Sundays and Bank Holidays,*

**St. Dunstan's-in-the-West**

**St. Paul's Cathedral**

*and there is an admission charge for visiting the interior, so if paying to see the very attic where the ubiquitous Dr. Johnson composed his famous dictionary does not move you, retrace your steps back to Fleet Street immediately.*

*When you get back to Fleet Street, turn left to the next traffic light, then cross back over to the south side of the street. A sign for* **Bouverie Street** *should be visible just to your right. Move into the street. The critic William Hazlitt lived at Number 3, (no longer here, but the site is marked by a blue plaque about shoulder high). A little farther down on the left (about where a high walkway over the street is located) is Magpie Alley.* This basic area was once a part of the Whitefriar's Monastery and somewhere near Magpie Alley was the small theatre called the Whitefriars that we alluded to a few paragraphs ago. It appears to have been a private theatre built within the refectory hall of the old monastery. The entire building was approximately 35 feet wide and 85 feet long. Little is known about it, but the Children of the King's and Queen's Revels

**5**

Top: Statue of Dr. Samuel Johnson
Bottom: Home of Dr. Johnson

played there under their director Philip Rosseter. Rosseter apparently left to take another hall in 1614. Lady Elizabeth's Men and later on the Prince's Men struggled on at the theatre until 1629. Samuel Pepys records a visit there in 1660, but he may have meant the Salisbury Court, which had opened nearby.

Residents of the Whitefriars precinct objected strenuously to the presence of actors and entertainments. They felt that the theatre attracted rough and unsavory people into the district and also created massive traffic jams in the narrow streets.

*Move along now to the intersection of* **Tudor Street** *where a glance to the right will reveal the third (eastern) entrance to the Inner Temple. Our route takes us to the left on Tudor Street.* John Dryden (1631-1700) lived along here as did the minor dramatist Thomas Shadwell (1642-1692). Shadwell wrote a play called *The Squire of Alsatia* in 1688 in which he took his characters from the low life types that lived around his house.

*Move along Tudor Street for two blocks until you reach John Carpenter Street. Take a right turn. On your left is a new monolithic grey stone building that houses the Morgan Guaranty and Trust, an American bank. The older building on the right is the former home of the Guildhall School of Music and Drama, which has now taken up new facilities in the Barbican Arts Complex. If you look closely at the facade of the building you will see a series of classical composers' names staring rather incongruously down into the street.* Busts used to occupy the empty circles below the names.

It is of course theatre and not music that brings us here. There used to be a nice blue plaque on the wall of an old London school that stood here before J. P. Morgan invaded. It announced that this was the site of the Dorset Garden Theatre (1671-1706). Plans for this famous and historic theatre were initiated by Sir William Davenant, who, along with Thomas Killigrew, held one of the two patents for dramatic performances issued by Charles II when he returned to the English throne in 1660. The ground was leased in 1670 and tradition indicates that Sir Christopher Wren was hired to design it. Davenant died before its completion and his widow and a group of investors headed by the actor Thomas Betterton finished and opened it in 1671. Betterton went on to manage the theatre for a number of years and actually lived in a flat on the premises.

According to all accounts, the Dorset Garden was the most lovely and fashionable theatre of its time. Several prints of its proscenium facade and 140 by 57 foot exterior are available. One of its most attractive features was the fine river frontage and private landing stage built to enable patrons to arrive and depart by boat, thus avoiding the

**5**

**Guildhall School of Music and Drama**

crowded and dangerous streets of the area. *Today if you look for a block or so on down John Carpenter Street you can make out the line of buildings that mark the river. That bright gold "Sea Container's House" sign that you can see is actually on the other side of the Thames.* If you had been standing here in 1671, you would be poised on top of the Dorset Stairs with the muddy banks of the Thames at your very feet. The difference is that in the 19th century the Victoria Embankment was constructed and the extensive tidal mud flats of river were claimed for a roadway and new buildings.

With Betterton as manager the Duke's Company at the Dorset Garden provided stiff competition for the Drury Lane company until 1682. At that time the two groups combined and moved into the more commodious Drury Lane Theatre. From then on the fortunes of the Dorset Garden receded and it was demolished sometime early in the 18th century.

**5**

*Turn around now and return to Tudor Street. Turn right for about 20 yards and then jog left on **Dorset Rise**. Climb the hill until you reach a small square with a signpost that says Bridewell Theatre on it. Turn around and look back. You should see a sign that says Salisbury Square. Walk back down to that sign and peek around it and to the left. There you should discover one of the most carefully hidden blue plaques in London.*

The Salisbury Court Theatre was built in 1629 as a private theatre and cost only 1000 pounds as compared to the Dorset Garden's 8000 pounds. It was on a site 140 by 40 feet and was initially occupied by the King's Revels (1629-31). Prince Charles' Men were there from 1631-35, and the Queen's Men from 1637-42. Apparently some clandestine performances were given there after the closure of the theatres in 1642. In 1649 its interior fittings were destroyed by soldiers,

but it was restored to usable condition by William Beeson in 1660. Beeson's own company used it briefly and then a group of players led by George Jolly. Jolly had toured in Germany during the Commonwealth and had also managed to perform before the future Charles II and secure a special licence to do plays in London should Charles ever be able to regain the throne. Davenant and Killigrew, however (see Walk 3), outmaneuvered poor old Jolly after 1660 and he ended up fading out of the picture even before the Great Fire of 1666 burned The Salisbury Court to the ground.

*Turn around again and make your way back into Salisbury Square. On your right is the entrance to St. Bride's Passage. Step through it and into a small courtyard. At the far end, on the site of Henry VIII's Bridewell Palace, is the 1893 building of the St. Bride Foundation Institute.* This was apparently a typical Victorian charity dedicated to providing both physical and intellectual stimulation to area residents. In 1994 the basement of this building was converted into the Bridewell Theatre. Doesn't sound too odd yet does it? Just wait. The basement of the building contained swimming baths. They were used until the 1950s. After thirty years of collecting dust the pool was remodeled into a theatre. On Walk Four we learned that the Savoy Theatre had a pool on top of it; now we have a theatre in one.

**Bridewell Theatre**

*Unless you feel compelled to examine it, turn around and step back out of the courtyard. Turn right and a few more steps will bring you to St. Bride's Avenue.* Samuel Pepys, the great diarist, was born in a house nearby. *Turn right into this passage and go through an anachronistic set of modern plate glass doors. You will find yourself in the **Church of St. Bride**, burned in the 1660s, rebuilt by Wren in the 1670s, bombed to a smoking shell in the 1940s, and restored again in the 1950s. As you enter take a long look at the "statues" of Moses and Aaron high up on the rear wall behind the altar. Then walk up close to it for a theatrical surprise courtesy of the artist Glyn Jones.*

The history of this exquisite Wren church is told eloquently in the basement museum. Theatrically we can mention that Thomas Sackville, co-author of that unreadable tragedy *Gorboduc,* was buried in an older church on the site and our friend Samuel Pepys and all of his brothers and sisters, who were born just a few steps away, were baptized in the old church.

*Leave St. Bride's by the north exit rather than the glass doors. A tiny remnant of the graveyard is to the right. Go straight ahead and out the entrance gates. When you arrive at **Fleet Street** take another look back and up at Wren's lacy spire. It is his tallest at 226 feet.*

**Church of St. Bride**

*Cross the busy street and turn left on the opposite side. About 150 yds back up Fleet Street is a major London tourist attraction,* **Ye Olde Cheshire Cheese,** *an inn and restaurant that was rebuilt in 1667 after the great fire and survives today with a good deal of its 17th century atmosphere intact, was much frequented by Dr. Samuel Johnson, James Boswell, and most of the literary figures of the day. The entrance is around the corner in* **Wine Office Court.** Johnson's own chair is even exhibited, but that particular item may just belong in the category with pieces of the true cross and beds that George Washington slept in. Despite the excess of tourists, it's worth a stop. Food is a bit dear for an academic's blood, but the price of a pint will give you access to the ambience.

*After your visit to the Cheshire Cheese, return to Fleet Street, cross over to the other side again, turn left, and continue on down toward the main intersection at the bottom of the hill. Once at the corner you are on the banks of what was a stinking ditch and open sewer until the latter part of the 18th century when the Fleet River was finally arched over and turned literally into what it had already become.*

*To your left up* **Farringdon Street** *you can just see the cast iron arches of the* **Holborn Viaduct,** *which was constructed in 1863 to carry traffic over the course of the river. Kitty corner across the road is the Old King Lud Pub.* Its recent renovation has destroyed most of its old character, but it is an apt reminder that you are approaching the old Lud Gate out of the City of London.

*Behind the Old King Lud on what would have been the opposite bank of the Fleet River would have stretched the sinister walls of the* **Fleet Prison.** Its existence has been traced back to the 11th century. It was continually destroyed and then rebuilt until it was finally pulled down for good in 1846. Its primary occupants were petty criminals and debtors. We have a vivid portrait of its 18th century interior in Hogarth's "Rake's Progress" paintings and a slightly different rendering of the prison by Charles Dickens, who placed Mr. Pickwick there for debt in the 19th century. The playwrights Thomas Dekker (1572-1632) and Thomas Nash (1567-1601) spent time there. William Wycherley (1640-1716) was imprisoned there for debt for seven full years.

*To your right down New Bridge Street toward the Thames was located another equally infamous prison—***Bridewell.** Thomas Kyd (1558-94), the author of the most popular and influential Elizabethan play of the 16th century, *The Spanish Tragedy,* was imprisoned and tortured there as a result of his connection to the playwright Christopher Marlowe. In May of 1593 constables searching for the authors of verses written against the immigration of Flemish Protestants searched Kyd's rooms and found instead some items that seemed to point to the even greater crimes of blasphemy, atheism, and other political and religious

**5**

heresy. Kyd, who was rooming with Marlowe at the time, was arrested and under torture attributed the authorship of the incriminating papers to his flatmate. Marlowe was then arrested, but he had better political connections and was released on bail. Unfortunately for Kyd, Marlowe was killed in a tavern brawl a month later and the affair was never resolved, though recent historical research suggests he was the victim of a deliberate political murder. Kyd remained imprisoned in Bridewell and was a broken man by the time he was finally released. He died in total poverty within a year. Thus it was that two of the finest and most promising young playwrights of Elizabethan England left a fast-growing, talent-hungry, and beckoning theatre scene to a young "Shakescene" in the early 1590s. Fictional treatments of this marvelous and mysterious story have tempted several authors. Try reading Anthony Burgess' *A Dead Man in Deptford* or Robin Chapman's *Christoferus* or Tom Kyd's *Revenge*.

**5**

*It is now time to make the last leg of our journey. Cross **Ludgate Circus** and begin your climb back up the opposite bank of the Fleet River onto **Ludgate Hill**, imagining as you do that you are exiting the City of London through the old Lud Gate. The gate actually stood somewhere between here and the **St. Martin Without Ludgate Church** which is just ahead on the left side of the street. As you climb the hill you might turn back and take another glance at the frosty white spire of St. Bride's behind you.* A baker named William Rich had a shop on this hill in the 18th century and is said to have modeled the wedding cakes he baked on the steeple he could see from his shop window. It began a style that is still followed today.

*Stop and visit St. Martin's Church. It is normally open.* William Penn, founder of Pennsylvania, was married in an older building on the same site. Just behind the church is the Stationer's Hall. This guild or company (founded in 1402) was given a royal charter in copywright. Until 1911 every book published in Britain had to be registered at the Hall. A good deal of our hard knowledge about Elizabethan literature and drama comes from the *Stationers' Register* that was kept by this guild. Their hall is not open to visitors.

*You have now reached the top of Ludgate Hill and one of the great symbols of London awaits your exploration. Theatrical names are not associated in any great numbers with **St. Paul's Cathedral** although its architect, Sir Christopher Wren, designed both the Second Drury Lane and the Dorset Garden theatres.* Hard by the walls of the cathedral and close to the Stationer's Company were the offices and shops of the major printers and publishers. The first edition of Shakespeare's *Venus and Adonis* and *The Rape* *of Lucrece* as well as the quartos of some of his plays were all published by printers working under the shadow of the (old) cathedral.

*Our walk ends here with the hope that you will now visit the masterpiece of Sir Christopher Wren. If you arrive before 3:30 PM (the crypt usually closes then) be sure to visit Wren's tomb, where one of the most moving epitaphs ever composed is found. It says:*

> Lector, si Momentum, requiris, circumspice
> (Reader, if you seek a monument, look about you.)

Since you are seldom out of sight of one of Wren's creations in London, it is more than fitting. The Cathedral has been the setting for the theatre of great national events—from the state funerals of the Duke of Wellington in 1852 and Sir Winston Churchill in 1965, to the wedding of Prince Charles and Princess Diana in 1981.

*After exploring St. Paul's, leave by the same exit you entered, turn right and walk parallel to the north side of the cathedral on Paternoster Row until you reach **Cheapside**. The **St. Paul's Tube Station** (Central Line) will be on your left.*

**5**

# WALK SIX

# PICK A DAFFY IN PICCADILLY AND BEYOND

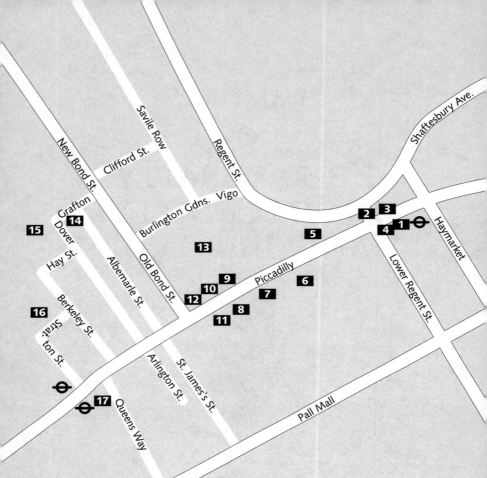

## Walk Six

1 Piccadilly Circus Tube Station
2 Piccadilly Circus
3 Eros Statue
4 Criterion Theatre
5 Meridien Hotel
6 St. James's Church
7 Hatchard's
8 Fortnum & Mason
9 Albany Courtyard
10 Burlington House; Royal Academy
11 Piccadilly Arcade
12 Burlington Arcade
13 Former Museum of Mankind
14 Medici Galleries
15 Berkeley Square
16 Mayfair Hotel; Mayfair Theatre
17 Green Park Tube Station
⊖ Tube Station

**STARTING POINT:** Piccadilly Circus Tube Station (Piccadilly or Bakerloo Lines). Many bus lines will also deposit you at Piccadilly Circus.

**APPROXIMATE TIME:** One and one-half hours.

T*his walk covers mainly vanished theatrical pleasures, but you will visit a nice variety of busy shops as well as the classy and quieter district known as Mayfair. Potential visits include Fortnum and Mason's, the Royal Academy, and the Medici Galleries. Schedule this one for a regular shopping day (Monday through Saturday) and do not start before 10:00 AM.*

W*e begin this walk at **Piccadilly Circus**, the hub of London's West End. If your arrival is by tube, look for an exit labeled Subway Four after you have cleared the ticket gates. Once in that subway you will see some stairs labeled **Shaftesbury Avenue** on your right. Go right on by and keep look-ing for a sign saying **Haymarket** and **Eros**. This stairway will deposit you above ground at a point convenient to the famous fountain with its graceful archer that has been casting its spell over the crowds since 1893.* Several generations of hopeful romantics have insisted upon calling the figure Eros, but it was actually intended to represent the Angel

of Christian Charity and to memorialize the phil-anthropy of Lord Shaftesbury—a 19th century industrial re-former and evangelical.

You can remember the true honoree if you note the direction the arrow has flown. i.e. Shaft's buried in ground thus Shaftes-bury. Unfortunately the missile is heading more toward Lower Regent Street than Shaftesbury Avenue, so it doesn't help your geographical orientation at all.

**Shaftesbury Avenue**

6

As you scan the square from the fountain search for the marquee of the **Criterion Theatre,** the only legitimate theatre remaining on Picadilly Circus. It is just to the left of Lillywhites. The frontage is unassuming but pleasant with the name picked out in white letters on blue tiles. Notice also the grotesque comic mask that crowns the marquee. *Cross toward it now.* It is London's only completely underground West End Theatre. When you are in the stalls the tube trains literally run beside you and even the upper circle is reached by going downstairs. The house,

**Above: Criterion Theatre entrance**
**Below: Criterion Theatre interior tilework**

which holds fewer than six hundred, is warm and intimate. The decor is soft pink and gold and the graceful curves of the circles are pleasantly

sinuous. The foyer and stairs have been enhanced with exquisite tile-work by William De Morgan, some of which is visible from the entrance hall. Small cast dramas, comedies, and revues have been its usual fare. Its long run champion is Ray Cooney's *Run For Your Wife,* which notched over 1,600 performances beginning in 1983. Other successes have been Terence Rattigan's first play, *French Without Tears,* Iris Murdoch's *A Severed Head,* Simon Gray's *Butley,* and Alan Ayckbourn's *Absurd Person Singular.* More important from a theatrical history standpoint might be the fact that Peter Hall's landmark production of Samuel Beckett's *Waiting For Godot* transferred here in 1955 from the Arts Theatre and went on to run for a full year. It went dark for a period in the early 1990s for a major redecoration, and just before it reopened to audiences it was the location for Kenneth Branagh's film of Chekhov's *Swansong,* starring John Gielgud and Richard Briers.

*If you have peeked into the Criterion's lobby, turn left upon exiting and cross **Lower Regent Street** toward the ABC Cinema to reach the south side of **Piccadilly**. On your right, across the street, are the flags and marquee of the **Meridien Hotel**.*

*If you could put yourself into the 19th century you might be able to conjure up an image of Charles Dickens striding up this street and entering St. James's Hall in 1870 to deliver his last public reading. That hall stood where the hotel stands today.*

Or you might imagine a jaunty Oscar Wilde parading up the avenue, then through Knightsbridge to Belgravia, where the actress Lillie Langtry lived. Wilde is purported to have carried a lily, symbol of the "Aesthetic Movement" and of Miss Langtry's name, on these journeys. In Gilbert and Sullivan's operetta *Patience,* which poked fun at the "Aesthetic Movement," the character Reginald Bunthorne was patterned after Wilde and one of the lyrics goes:

> Though philistines may jostle
> You will rank as an apostle
> In the high aesthetic band
> If you walk down Piccadilly
> With a poppy or a lily
> In your Medieval hand.

You may not be carrying a lily today in honor of Oscar Wilde, but you will certainly be jostled on these busy sidewalks. *On past the hotel there will shortly appear on your left the thin rapier-like spire of Christopher Wren's **St. James's Church**.* Its particular theatre connection is that it has become the most favored venue now for actors' and writers' memorial services.

*When you leave the churchyard, turn left and continue your perambulation past the offices of BAFTA—the British Academy of Film and Television Arts, to the façade of one of London's oldest **booksellers—Hatchards**.* They have been in business since 1797 and in that building

**St. James's Church**

since 1801. If they are open, there is no penalty for taking a look.

*A bit further on is the home of* **Fortnum and Mason,** *where some of the most elegant foodstuffs in the world can be found.* A visit should be mandatory, if only to see the staff in their morning coats and to register shock at the prices.

*When you come back out, cross Piccadilly and turn right, until you reach* **Albany Court,** *directly opposite Hatchards Bookshop. Find it and go in. At the rear of the courtyard is the entrance to the luxury lodgings known as Albany.* They were created within the framework of an earlier house designed in the 1770s by Sir William Chambers. *What was built in 1802 was a row of apartments all facing onto a long covered passage, called The Ropewalk, that passed all the way through to Vigo Street and Burlington Gardens.\* If the door is open you can see the long line of delightful columns clearly.* It has been and continues to be a most desirable address. Theatrical occupants have included Dion Boucicault, the prolific author/adaptor of at least 150 plays including *The Corsican Brothers* (1852), *The Octoroon* (1859) and *London Assurance,* which was first performed in 1841 and memorably revived by the RSC at the Aldwych in 1970, with Donald Sinden and Judi Dench; the playwright, J.B. Priestley; the actor/manager Herbert Beerbohm-Tree; and the playwright, Henry Arthur Jones. Other famous residents have included Lord Byron, William Gladstone, Aldous Huxley, and Graham Greene. *Return to Piccadilly and turn right.*

\*According to a recent book by Ann Saunders, The Art and Architecture of London, a man by the name of Alexander Copeland did the conversion work on Albany apartments. Other sources indicated that Henry Holland, the architect of the third Drury Lane Theatre, designed the conversion.

**Above: Albany**
**Below: Burlington House**

*Immediately the massive gates of* **Burlington House,** *a 17th century Palladian villa that now houses the Royal Academy, come into view.*

Major art exhibitions are mounted here throughout the year and the current show is usually advertised prominently. *Walk into the courtyard and take a peek at the statue of its first President, Sir Joshua Reynolds, while you make up your mind whether a visit is in order.*

*Turn right as you exit from the* **Royal Academy courtyard.** *Note just across the street is the entrance to the* **Piccadilly Arcade.** *This is the*

*former site of the Egyptian Hall. No's 170-173 just beyond the Arcade are still labeled Egyptian House.* There is a bizarre story connected with this place. It seems that an obscure painter by the name of Benjamin Haydon had a display of his work in a front gallery of this hall in 1846. Unfortunately the central part of the hall was hired by the great showman P. T. Barnum, who was exhibiting his famous dwarf General Tom Thumb. This event so submerged Haydon's exhibition that the distraught artist cut his throat three months later. The Great Showman may not have been much of an art critic but he clearly knew what an audience would buy.

*If you are standing directly across from the **Piccadilly Arcade**, you are about twenty paces from the entrance to the **Burlington Arcade**.* Dating from 1818, it was built originally as a buffer to keep the riffraff from throwing trash into Lord Burlington's elegant gardens. Today it's the prices that keep the riffraff away. *Turn to your right into the arcade and take a leisurely stroll into the past. Keep an eye out for the top hatted and waistcoated Burlington Beadles with their amusingly anachronistic two-way radios.* They were formed to protect the customers and to keep them faithful to the laws of Regency London. They may legally forbid you to whistle, sing, or hurry. And hurry we certainly do not want you to do. The shops are little theatrical jewels in and of themselves and deserve to be savored even if you cannot afford to buy.

As you come up on the far end of the arcade note the two sturdy posts set in the top step. Early one morning in 1964 a blue Jaguar jumped the curb and roared down the deserted arcade. It screamed to a stop at Goldsmith's Jewelers, some men leaped out, and sixty seconds later sped off toward the Piccadilly entrance with 150,000 pounds' worth of loot. The posts may not prevent another theft, but the next getaway vehicle will have to be on two wheels.

**Piccadilly Arcade**

**Former Museum of Mankind**

**6**

 *The street at the top of the arcade is* **Burlington Gardens,** *and if you turn to the right you will walk past the imposing building that used to house the* **Museum of Mankind.** This ethnographic collection has now been moved back to the British Museum in Bloomsbury. *A bit farther on is the rear entrance to the Albany and then Savile Row, the famous street of quality tailors. Turn left there and look for Number 14, the plain but sturdy Georgian house where the playwright Richard Brinsley Sheridan lived.* It is only barely marked with a dim brown plaque above the Hardy Amies sign on the doorway. Number 17, a few doors down, is also an attractive building in spite of the addition of wrought iron trim from another period. Sheridan died in 1816 in the front bedroom of this house, though the blue plaque commemorates the much less well-known architect, George Basevi, 1794-1845.

 *You are now almost to* **Clifford Street.** *When you reach, it turn left.*

**Richard Brinsley Sheridan house**

**Bronzes of Winston Churchill and Franklin Roosevelt**

**6**  *There are some lovely Georgian houses along this street. Number 8, on your right, is particularly fine. Walk three short blocks to **New Bond Street**, then take a jog left. Stop and be pleasantly amazed, for sitting quietly on a park bench are lifesize bronzes of Winston Churchill and Franklin Roosevelt.* Haul out your camera and have someone take a few snaps of you hobnobbing with your famous friends. You will see where to perch by the highly-polished left knee of Roosevelt and right elbow of Churchill. *After you finish take a quick right into **Grafton***

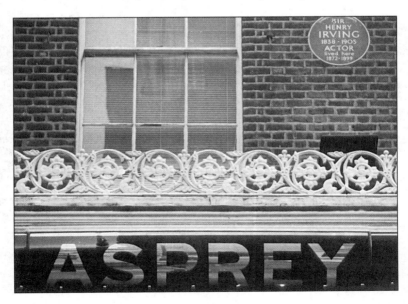

**Street.** *On the corner at 15A (the ground floor is now the premises of Asprey's, the famous jewelry store) lived the greatest of the 19th century actor/managers, Sir Henry Irving. You'll see a blue plaque there.* He occupied his flat here for almost 30 years from 1872-1899.

*The right side of the street now contains a slim new grey marble office block, but at Number 13 (now the location of Wartski, jewelers of distinction) was the Albemarle Club.* It was here that the Marquess of Queensberry left a fateful note for Oscar Wilde. The allegations prompted Wilde to sue for defamation of character. He won this case but the publicity led to the morals charge, which ultimately sent him to prison and ruin.

*Continue on down Grafton Street until it takes a sharp left when it turns into* **Dover St.** *Huddled at the corner here are the main offices of the* **Medici Galleries**—*distributors of fine cards and prints.* You may wish to stop in and browse a bit. It is normally uncrowded and the staff are friendly.

*Upon coming out of the Medici Galleries follow Dover street one short block to* **Hay Hill.** *Turn right there and go down the hill to* **Berkeley Street.** This name is pronounced "BARK-LEE," by the way. *To your right is* **Berkeley Square,** *immortalized during World War II in a song by Vera Lynn entitled "A Nightingale Sang in Berkeley Square." Unless you feel a need for a rest turn left away from the square and walk on along* **Berkeley Street** *until you reach* **Stratton Street.** Just in case you hadn't realized it, you are now in Mayfair—a district of the city that Michael Elliot in *Heartbeat London* called "one of the bolt-holes of old money." *Take a right past the "posh"* **Mayfair Intercontinental Hotel.** *As you walk under the main marquee there is a glass door on your right labeled* **Mayfair Theatre.** This pleasant and well-equipped 300-seat house was constructed inside the Candlelight Ballroom of the hotel. It opened in 1963 with a highly successful production of Pirandello's *Six Characters in Search of an Author* starring Ralph Richardson. It housed Christopher Hampton's *The Philanthropist* in the 1970s; a thriller entitled *The Business of Murder* had a five-year run in the 1980s; but in recent years it seems to have been more in use for conferences than for the dramatic arts.

*A bit farther along on Stratton Street at Number 17 is a five-story red brick building tucked in among more modern neighbors. Henry Irving occupied rooms here briefly in 1900 and James Barrie lived in the building in 1908.*

*Stratton Street then curls back to Piccadilly and the Green Park tube station. You can terminate your stroll here or walk back down to*

**6**

*Piccadilly Circus stopping at places you may have passed up on the out-bound journey. Another alternative is to go on to Walk Seven— "From St. James to the Haymarket." It originates at the Green Park under-ground station and takes you back to Piccadilly Circus via a somewhat more theatrical route.*

**6**

**Henry Irving and James Barrie occupied rooms here.**

# WALK SEVEN

# Clubland is also Playland:
## from St. James to the Haymarket

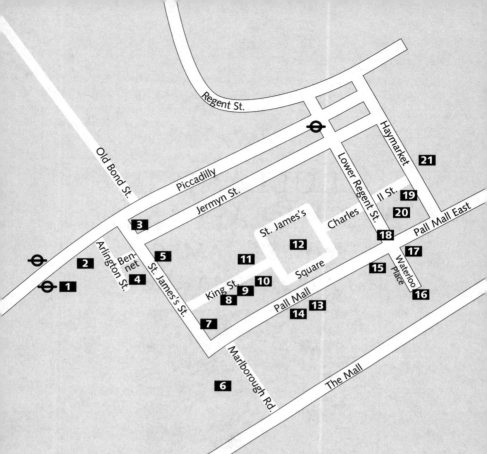

### Walk Seven

1 Green Park Station
2 Ritz Hotel
3 White's
4 Brooks Club
5 Boodle's
6 St. James's Palace
7 Berry Brothers & Rudd;
 Lock & Company, Hatters
8 St. James's House
9 Angel Court
10 Golden Lion
11 Christie's
12 St. James's Square
13 Royal Automobile Club
14 Peninsular House
15 Reform Club; Travelers
 Club; Athenaeum Club
16 Duke of York monument
17 Institute of Directors
18 Crimean War Memorial
19 Her Majesty's Theatre
20 Royal Opera Arcade
21 Haymarket Theatre
⊖ Tube Station

This walk takes you past a royal palace, several old London clubs, the site of the historic St. James Theatre, and finally closes with a look at two of the West End's best known theatres—Her Majesty's and the Haymarket.

Take the underground to Green Park (Victoria or Piccadilly Line). You will emerge from the **Green Park Tube Station** onto **Piccadilly** and must locate on the south side the grey bulk and covered arcades of the **Ritz Hotel,** where afternoon tea is still a production number.

If you are continuing on from Walk Six, you will end at the entrance to the Green Park Station and need only look across the street to find the Ritz. Cross busy Piccadilly and walk along the side of the hotel under the arches. Visit the lobby if you are reasonably well dressed. Go past **Arlington Street** and on to **St. James's Street**. Take a peek in the windows at the Caviar House on the corner.

When you reach St. James's Street, turn right and let your eye roam down one of London's most pleasant streetscapes. Within a scant third of a mile you have a wealth of artistic, political, commercial, and social history. Since the 18th century this street has been the heart of London clubland.

As you start down the hill, the second building on your left from the corner is **White's,** the oldest London Club, founded in 1693. (You will soon observe that none of the long-established gentlemen's clubs do anything so vulgar as to put their name on their door). The present building dates from the 1750s and contains a famous bow window on the first floor that should be of some interest to costumiers. It was there that Beau Brummell and his friends displayed themselves in the garb that set the fashions for the day. Colley Cibber, the 18th century actor and theatre manager, was a member of White's. His interest to theatre

**The Ritz**

**White's**

**7**

historians now is that he added some embellishments of his own to Shakespeare's *Richard III*, a couple of which Laurence Olivier included in his film portrayal: "Off with his head, so much for Buckingham," and on the morning after the King's nightmare, "Richard's himself again." Edmund Kean was famous for his effects with these interpolated lines, and Olivier was not averse to following his example, though none of the film critics appeared to notice.

*Continue walking and pass* **Bennet Street.** *A bit further along on your right, just past number 60, is* **Brooks Club,** *founded in 1764.* The current building dates from 1788. Richard Brinsley Sheridan and David Garrick were both members of Brooks, as were men like Edmund Burke, David Hume, Sir Robert Walpole, Charles James Fox, and Sir Joshua Reynolds.

**Brooks Club**

**St. James's Palace**

On the left side of the street, across and back a bit from Brooks, at Number 28, is **Boodles** (white stucco ground floor and brick above) founded in 1762 and in this building since 1783. The building is more airy and gracious than Brooks. Several other clubs occupy premises on the right side all the way down to **St. James's Palace** (home of the Queen Mother) at the far end of the street. By the way, if you want to see a mini changing of the guard up close and don't want to fight the crowds at Buckingham Palace, station yourself in the St. James's Palace courtyard. Check a current guide for the times.

When you reach the beginning of **Pall Mall** at the bottom of St. James's Street, cross over and wander back up the other side. There you will find some of London's most venerable and exclusive shops. Number 3 is **Berry Brothers & Rudd**, wine merchants. Just past their shop, you should see the tiny passage called Pickering Place. Nothing theatrical down there, but it is an enchanting little nook and also the spot where the fledgling Republic of Texas had their official ambassadorial digs from 1842-1845.

Number 6, **Lock & Company, Hatters**, always has an extraordinary display of specialized headgear. Number 9 is John Lobb, Bootmaker.

**Berry Brothers & Rudd**

*Lobb's has an interesting display of period footwear, including the very lasts used to make Queen Victoria's shoes. Construction is done right in the front of the shop and you can watch their craftsmen work on handmade boots just as they have for two hundred years.*

*Continue to walk back up the hill until you reach **King Street**. Then turn right. If curiosity gets you, turn right off King Street into gaslit Crown Passage. There are a number of little shops, sandwich bars, and even a pub called The Red Lion tucked away down there. They are primarily for the locals and reasonably priced.*

*If Crown Passage doesn't call, continue on down King Street to Number 23-24 where you will find **St. James's House.*** The name calls up a sad little reminder of the all but forgotten St. James's Theatre. It was built on this site in 1835 by Mr. John Braham, a well known tenor and good friend of Charles Dickens.

**Lobb craftsman works in the window**

7

At one point, in the lobby of the current St. James's House, you could find a handsome bound volume that preserved pictures and programs from the old theatre. It was also possible to obtain from the security guard a small self-congratulatory pamphlet that described the new building that replaced the theatre. The document proudly proclaimed that "the actual site of the stage was now a balcony at the south end of the staff restaurant." How's that for respectful veneration of the past? By the late 1980s a functionary at the door of the building could only produce a badly photocopied version of the original bound scrapbook.

In 1994 the photocopy had disappeared and the frosted glass panel above the door is apparently an attempt to introduce a ghost image of the past into the present structure. At the top of the panel is an image derived from a sculpted figure of Fame that appeared above the stage of the old theatre, flanked by two unexplained winged beasts. The side panels are meant to portray a metaphoric family group looking toward fame, and an abstracted curtain with various symbols of culture and business is intended to convey a sense of the international cross-fertilization of commerce and art.

*At this point you need to walk on a few steps further and find a small alleyway opening, just past a ramp leading down to the parking garage entrance. This is called* **Angel Court.** *Walk down this alley about fifty yards looking on your right for three slabs of stone mounted on a wall over the point where the parking ramp enters the building.* These slabs are three bas-relief panels commemorating people who contributed to the noble history of the St. James's Theatre. They used to decorate the front of the 1960 building that replaced the demolished theatre, and have now been moved to their present point of prominence. *Get to a position where you can see the panels.*

The top panel honors Sir George Alexander, the actor-producer, who was in charge of the theatre from 1892 to 1918. His sculpted head is flanked by figures from two of his most famous roles in *The Prisoner of Zenda* and *If I Were a King.*

The middle panel alludes to Alexander's premiere productions in the theatre of Oscar Wilde's *Lady Windermere's Fan* and *The Importance of Being Earnest* in 1892 and 1895 respectively. For some reason known only to the sculptor, Wilde's portrait is flanked by representations of Dorian Gray and Salome rather than figures from the two famous plays associated with the theatre. Other important first nights during this period were Arthur Wing Pinero's *The Second Mrs. Tanqueray* and George Bernard Shaw's *Androcles and the Lion.*

The bottom panel depicts Mr. Gilbert Miller who acquired the theatre lease in 1918 and managed it throughout the twenties and thirties when a galaxy of West End stars paraded across its boards. A quick sampling of names would include Sybil Thorndike, Edith Evans, Claude Rains, Noel Coward, Cedric Hardwicke, The Lunts, Gerald du Maurier, and Gladys Cooper. Miller went on to buy the theatre outright after the Second World War and controlled its fortunes up until it was sold for re-development in 1954.

*At this time turn around and go back toward King Street. Just before you reach the street you enter a small covered area containing some tables for the pub next door. On the wall of this little nook you will find a brown wooden plaque commemorating the St. James's Theatre, put up by the*

*City of Westminster and the Society of West End Theatres. Set in the wall
above it is a fourth bas-relief stone frieze, featuring the heads of Laurence
Olivier and Vivien Leigh, flanked by full-length figures of them as Antony
and Cleopatra.*

The Oliviers took out a four-year lease on the St. James's Theatre
in 1949 with the idea of restoring the grand old 19th century
actor/manager tradition. The figures on the ends of the frieze honor
the successful 1951 Festival of Britain productions in which Olivier
and Leigh appeared alternately in Shaw's *Caesar and Cleopatra* and
Shakespeare's *Antony and Cleopatra*. The double bill transferred to
Broadway to great acclaim. Unfortunately the management venture
proved unsuccessful and the theatre went dark. There was a last ditch
campaign to save the theatre from the wrecking ball in 1957. Vivien
Leigh led the public demonstrations against its closure, including a
solo protest from the Visitors' Gallery of the House of Lords which
captured the front pages of the newspapers, but it was not enough
to save it and London lost another piece of its glorious theatre past.

*Before leaving you should take a bit of refreshment and a short tour
of the Golden Lion pub.* It has been here long enough to preserve
signs of its lost theatrical neighbor. There are little tragic and comic
masks in its leaded glass windows. The stairs to the second floor and
the luncheon room above are decorated with prints and programs
associated with the St. James's.

*Upon leaving the pub turn right. At or around number 26 (now a
construction site) once stood Mr. William Almack's Assembly Rooms.*
From 1705 until 1863, this semi-auditorium was the home of fashionable fine arts, music and drama soirées. *We should probably also mention that opposite Angel Court is the home, since 1823, of the famous
auction house, Christie's. Drama of another kind goes on there daily.
The sale rooms are open to the public and may be visited.*

*Moving along King Street you will soon come to the green oasis of St.
James's Square. Move around the square clockwise. You are entering
at six o'clock and will be making an almost full circuit and leaving by
the exit at four o'clock.* It is hard to believe that not too long ago this
elegant and peaceful location was the scene of an international ter-
rorist incident. On April 17, 1984, demonstrators outside the Libyan
embassy (it was Number 5 in the eleven o'clock corner of the square)

were fired on from an embassy window. A British policewoman, Yvonne Fletcher, who was guarding the demonstrators, was shot and killed. After several days of negotiating, with the square completely cordoned off, the entire Libyan embassy staff, including the unidentified presumed killer, was escorted to the airport and deported. There is a moving little memorial to Fletcher on the inner corner of the square marking the spot where she was struck down.

*Those with less current historical interests may wish to stroll the perimeter of the square to admire the facades, including some by Adam and Hawksmoor. Along the way you should be able to see the Georgian townhouse of Mary Astor, the first woman member of the British Parliament, the house where three British Prime Ministers have lived (Chatham House) which now houses the Royal Institute of International Affairs, and General Dwight Eisenhower's World War II Allied forces headquarters (Norfolk House). Exit the square in the southeast corner at the four o'clock heading. Just a few steps and you will be on **Pall Mall**.*

*Across from you is the **Royal Automobile Club** building. Cross the street, turn to the right, and stroll along Pall Mall until you locate Number 79, **Peninsular House**. This 1890 office block now houses the P & O Steamship Line, but the blue plaque reminds us that in the 17th century this site contained the home of the Restoration actress, Nell Gwynn.* As Arthur Mee noted in his *London: The City and Westminster*, all of the south side of Pall Mall is crown property except for this tract. When Gwynn became Charles II's mistress, she insisted that she would not live in a house that was not her own and the king acceded to her demands and deeded the freehold over to her. Two other long-term mistresses of Charles II, the Duchess of Cleveland and the actress Moll Davis, also lived nearby.

There is much more to tell here, of course. The lovely Nellie lived at 79 Pall Mall from 1671 until her death and her house became one of the most convivial centers of London political and social life. Though she was never officially raised in status, both of her sons by Charles II were elevated to the peerage. One of them, the Duke of St. Albans, successfully negotiated the British political scene after his mother's death and was installed as a Knight of the Garter by George I. For the full story of this remarkable woman and actress, check out Roy MacGregor-Hastie's biography titled *Nell Gwynn*.

*Back across the street from where you are now standing was the bizarre Shakespeare Gallery of London alderman John Boydell.* He used a good share of his fortune to commission 18th century artists to paint and sculpt scenes from Shakespeare's plays. The gallery ended in failure, but the works commissioned for it continue to be exhibited throughout the country. For instance the well known Fuseli Shakespeare drawings, which were originally commissioned by Boydell, are now exhibited at the Tate Gallery.

*Reverse your steps and walk back down Pall Mall. You will repass on your right the Royal Automobile Club, then shortly the ornate classical bulk of the* **Reform Club** *(Number 104), then the more austere* **Travelers Club** *where the intrepid adventurer Phileas Fogg set out around the world in eighty days, and finally, at the corner of Pall Mall and Waterloo Place, the creamy stucco side of the* **Athenaeum Club** *(1830). Upon reaching Waterloo Place and the* **monument to The Duke of York,** *cross over the wide boulevard toward John Nash's 1827 United Services Club (now the* **Institute of Directors***) and turn back. The classical frieze by John Henning on the front of the Athenaeum Club can best be admired from here. To your right is* **Lower Regent Street** *heading back up toward* **Piccadilly.**

*Walk that direction, past the monument for the Crimean War dead, until you come to Charles II Street. Turn to your right here and focus on another lovely neoclassic city view planned and executed by the architect John Nash. Ahead of you at the far end of the street is the gleaming, columned, white facade of the* **Haymarket Theatre.**

Nash, (1752-1835), the dominant figure in Regency architecture, was the town planning genius who conceived the idea of linking London's West End with Regent's Park via the creation of Regent Street. *His serene style can also be seen on your right as you walk down Charles II Street. Look for, and explore if you wish, the entryway to the* **Royal Opera Arcade** *(1817) which recedes splendidly into the interior of New Zealand House in a series of graceful lighted domes and hanging flower baskets. Note the two old boot scrapers just inside to your right. Visit some of the*

**7**

Athenaeum Club

*pleasant and ever changing shops if you wish.*

*If you entered the arcade turn right when you re-emerge. Otherwise just continue to walk straight ahead on Charles II Street.*

Four different theatres have stood in the area just past the Royal Opera Arcade moving up toward Haymarket. The first of these was known as the Queen's Theatre and was built in 1705 by the playwright and architect, Sir John Vanbrugh. William Congreve was the first manager. It was a huge barn of a place and not too successful until 1709 when the acting company moved to the Drury Lane Theatre and the vacant theatre was taken over by the

**Haymarket Theatre**

**7**

producers of Italian opera. Thus it became the cradle of Italian opera in England and the first theatre in the country given over solely to opera production.

After a fire laid the first building to waste, a second and larger theatre took its place in 1791. A remodeling of that building in 1816 resulted in a classical colonnade on three sides with Nash's Royal Opera arcade built to occupy the fourth side. From 1830 to 1850 it was the musical social center of London. Fire took this building as well and in 1867 a third structure was erected. The next twenty years were checkered, but the theatre did see the London premiere of *Carmen* in 1878, the first complete performance of Wagner's *Ring* in England in 1882, and two Sarah Bernhardt tours in 1886 and 1890.

*As you finish your walk toward Haymarket now, you will be alongside the fourth theatre. At the corner you can turn right and view the facade of **Her Majesty's Theatre**, which was built in 1896 by the great actor-manager Sir Herbert Beerbohm-Tree.* Carrying on in the tradition of Henry Irving, Tree was also famous for lavishly mounted Shakespeare productions, with live rabbits in the Forest of Arden, and Richard II entering on a real horse. After his first performance as Hamlet, W. S. Gilbert said to Tree, "My dear fellow, I never saw anything so funny in my life, and yet it was not in the least vulgar." Irving's own view of Tree's clear ambition to succeed him as the pre-eminent actor-manager of the late Victorian era is best exemplified by their famous public encounter on this spot. Tree was simultaneously leasing the Haymarket Theatre and building Her Majesty's for his own use; viewing progress on the latter he was greeted by Sir Henry who said, "Mornin' Tree, working?" In 1904 Beerbohm Tree started a drama school in connection with his theatre. That school is still functioning, though not here, and is now known as The Royal Academy of Dramatic Art, commonly abbreviated to RADA.

The Tree tenure from 1897 to 1917 can make up a book alone, as indeed it has, and the stories abound. One of the most intriguing is that of Hubert Carter, a lumbering giant of a man, who was a supporting player for Tree over many years. According to MacQueen-Pope in his *Ghosts and Greasepaint,* Carter was famous throughout the town as a prodigious eater. He would buy two pounds of steak, have the butcher cube it, eat it raw right there on the spot, and then go in search of lunch. One of Carter's favorite roles was Claudius in *Hamlet.* His interpretation called for a fiercely masculine king and in marvelous pre-Method diligence he would purchase a pint of ox-blood before each night's performance and drink it down just before stepping on stage.

Another story told about him concerned a post-performance visit with a friend to an out-of-the-way pub. Immediately upon their entrance, Carter and his companion attracted the attention of the shady clientele. It was clear immediately that robbery, mayhem, or worse was being contemplated. Carter sized up the situation and strode over to the fireplace, picked a poker out of the grate, and bent it to the shape of a horseshoe. Then, smiling apologetically, he bent it back straight again, and replaced it. He and his friend, unbothered, then finished their drink calmly and left.

**7**

In 1916 a show called *Chu Chin Chow* started a 2,238-performance string at Her Majesty's and that was London's long run champion until 1958 when it was passed by the current and still running champion, Agatha Christie's *The Mousetrap.* The post-war years saw the house occupied mainly by musicals, many of them from America, including *Brigadoon, West Side Story, Bye Bye Birdie, Fiddler on the Roof,* and *Applause.* Since 1986 the theatre has been hosting the long running

**Her Majesty's Theatre**

production of Andrew Lloyd Webber's *The Phantom of the Opera*.

As important as the story of Her Majesty's is, it pales into insignificance, when compared with the history of The Haymarket Theatre, just across the street.

The first Haymarket, or Little Theatre in the Hay, was built in 1720 with the hope of breaking the royal patent monopoly that dated all the way back to Killigrew and Davenant in the Restoration. But this did not happen and the theatre operated on and off for the next fifteen years as a sort of fringe home for a potpourri of entertainments, some of them legal and some of them not.

In 1733 more notice came to the tiny theatre when Theophilus Cibber, son of the manager and comedian Colley Cibber, brought in a company of disgruntled actors who had revolted against the management of Drury Lane. The patent companies were becoming more than a little disturbed now and this turned to open warfare when the playwright Henry Fielding took over the managership in 1735. His lively, but crude, satires began to attract positive attention in the town and negative attention from some of the key politicians, who were the butts of Fielding's jokes. Sir Robert Walpole was particularly incensed. Before the fray was over, the Licensing Act of 1737 was on the books and Fielding decided that writing novels was a more promising field of endeavor than the theatre.

Briefly, the Licensing Act limited the number of theatres to those currently holding patents, required all new productions to get an authorization from the Lord Chamberlain, and gave the Lord Chamberlain power to prohibit any individual theatrical performance. We do not have time to deal with government censorship of the English theatre here, but suffice it to say that what was initiated primarily by the happenings at the Little Theatre in the Hay remained a part of English law until 1968, when the function of the Lord Chamberlain to approve manuscripts and license plays for performance was finally abolished.

The effect of the Licensing Act on the Haymarket was immediate and telling. It was closed and remained so for a good deal of the time over the next several years. Finally in 1747 a second-rate actor, Samuel Foote, gathered a company and reopened the building. His gambit to evade the licensing laws was to advertise the sale of tea or chocolate. Musical and dramatic entertainment just happened to be included in the price of the drinks. Things were still touch and go, however, and Foote finally got his official patent the hard way. While at a party he was boasting of his prowess as a horseman. The Duke of York was quick to produce a lively animal. Foote mounted, was thrown, and broke his leg in so many places that it had to be amputated. The contrite Duke offered a favor in order to make amends, and Foote asked for some intercession with the King to get a patent for the Haymarket. Thus in 1766 he was finally granted a licence to perform legally during the summers when the other theatres were closed. So in essence Foote got his patent as a result of a lucky break.

Many years later, in 1820, it was decided to rebuild the theatre as a part of John Nash's grand plan for the West End. It was moved a little to the south (the present position) in order to create a pleasing vista from St. James's Square down Charles II Street. It is that exterior, completed in 1821, that you still see today, making it the second oldest functioning theatre in the city. The interior has been completely renovated several times since then, with the present Louis XIV style dating from 1941.

It is impossible to catalog the list of famous productions and stars that have appeared at the Haymarket over the past 150 years. Even a limited list would have to be a very personal choice. There were Phelps, Macready, Tree, and Ellen Terry in the 19th century, along with plays by Tom Robertson, Shakespeare, and Wilde. In the early 20th century there was the first English production of Maeterlinck's *The Blue Bird;* the original scene designs for that production now decorate the walls of the Upper Circle Bar in the theatre. The year 1914 saw the first licensed public theatre performance of Ibsen's *Ghosts*. In 1944 there was a major repertory season under the direction of John Gielgud. In 1948 Helen Hayes made her first London appearance in Tennessee Williams's *The Glass Menagerie*. Other successes in recent years have included Thornton Wilder's *The Matchmaker, The Heiress, The Chalk Garden, Two for the Seesaw,* and any number of Shakespeare, Wilde, and Shaw revivals. The latter's *Heartbreak House* starring Paul Scofield, Vanessa Redgrave and Felicity Kendal was a sellout in 1992, and so was Tom Stoppard's *Arcadia* in 1994.

We shouldn't leave this historic site without mentioning Mr. John Buckstone, an actor and manager of the Haymarket from 1853 to 1878. His ghost still allegedly haunts the theatre and has been seen by many actors and stage personnel over the years. He is a benign presence and usually opens and shuts doors, walks the corridors, rests in dressing rooms, or sits quietly in the royal box. When Donald Sinden was a young actor he made his West End debut in the 1953 production of *The Heiress,* starring Ralph Richardson and Peggy Ashcroft. One night, descending the stairs from his dressing-room to the stage, he passed a frock-coated figure with his back to him. He said "Good evening Sir Ralph," but received no reply, and was astonished when he reached the wings to find that the great actor was already there, in an identical Victorian costume. He is convinced that as he bounded down the stairs the figure he had passed was the legendary ghost of Buckstone.

*Should you wish to look for him yourself, perhaps you should step across the street and purchase a ticket for the current production. Otherwise, a turn to your left and a short stroll will take you back to **Piccadilly Circus** and convenient transportation back to your hotel or flat.*

# WALK EIGHT

# LONG GONE BUT NOT FORGOTTEN:
## TOWER HILL TO ST. LEONARD SHOREDITCH

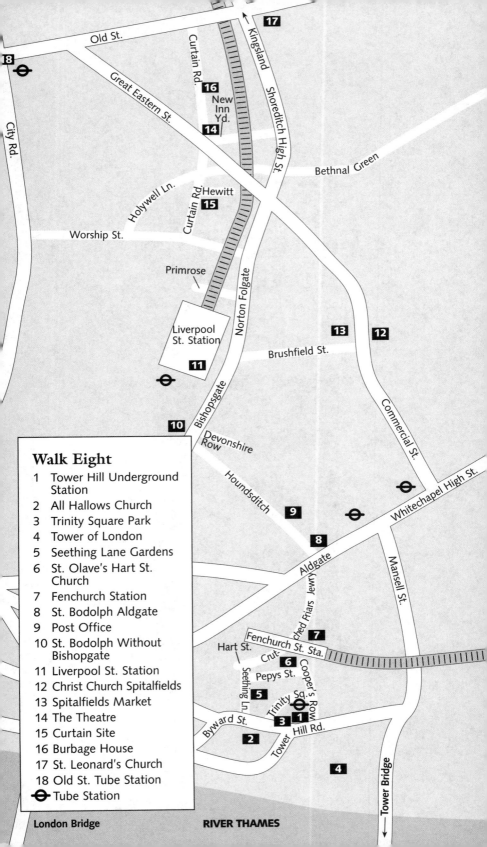

**Walk Eight**

Old St.

Great Eastern St.

Curtain Rd.

Kingsland

17

8

City Rd.

New Inn Yd.

16

14

Shoreditch High St.

Bethnal Green

Holywell Ln.

Curtain Rd. Hewitt

15

Worship St.

Primrose

Norton Folgate

Liverpool St. Station

11

Brushfield St.

13

12

Commercial St.

10

Bishopsgate

Devonshire Row

Houndsditch

Whitechapel High St.

9

8

Aldgate

Mansell St.

Crutched Friars

Jewry

7

Fenchurch St. Sta.

Hart St.

Crut.

6

Pepys St.

Seething Ln.

5

Cooper's Row

Byward St.

Trinity Sq.'s Row

3

1

2

Tower Hill Rd.

4

Tower Bridge

**London Bridge**          **RIVER THAMES**

**T**his walk is not the stuff that most tourist brochures are made of; it's gritty and traffic filled but it does include a visit to the site of "The Theatre" the first permanent professional public theatre in London. It is also intended to give you a sense of the kind of journey it would have taken to get to a performance. Along the way there are several other items of thespian interest.

**W**e start this ramble at the **Tower Hill underground station.** It would combine nicely with a visit to the Tower of London, which has inspired enough drama to qualify hands up as a premiere theatrical site. Our walk does grow out of the Tower's medieval heritage and also gives you a chance to get off the main tourist paths. This may be quite welcome if you have spent the morning amid the mobs fighting for your very own twenty-second view of the Crown Jewels.

*Walk dead ahead as you pass through the tube ticket machine and you should be able to see over the busy* **Tower Hill Road** *the copper green spire of a church called* **All Hallows by the Tower.** *That's where you are heading. Take a left at the iron fence and look for the gate into* **Trinity Square Park.** *Cross into the park, stop, and take in the vista. Across Tower Hill Road and a bit*

**All Hallows by the Tower**

8

113

**Tower of London**

*to the left is the **Tower of London** itself. To the right, dominating the quiet of Trinity Square Gardens is the rather vulgar bulk of the Port of London Authority building. And out in front of you is the church spire.*

*Step quietly along the walk through the Seaman's Memorial and remember that you are also quite near the site of the Tower Hill Scaffold where large numbers of the not so lucky met their maker.* It was regarded a privilege to be executed inside the Tower, where the public was normally barred and the victim, as William Chambers said, was spared the final indignity of having his head held aloft by the headsman who announced, "Behold the head of the traitor." Actually a majority of the condemned prisoners held at the Tower were dispatched at the public scaffold, including that man for all seasons Sir Thomas More. The short stairs leading to the gallows were apparently rickety and More is reputed to have said to the Lieutenant by his side, "See me safely up, for my coming down I can shift for myself."

*Exit the park on the opposite side toward the Allied Bank of Pakistan. Then jog left down **Trinity Square** and finally right into busy **Byward Street**. When you are about even with the church, a subway (underpass) should come up on your right. Use it to cross the road if you value your life.*

All Hallows by the Tower is an extremely old church with even older Roman paving stones in the crypt. From its tower (the current copper spire in the Wren style is post World War II), Samuel Pepys watched the Great Fire of London spread in 1666. The church was saved from the ravages of the fire by Admiral William Penn Sr., a parishioner and father of the founder of Pennsylvania. His young son William Jr. was baptized here in 1644. Penn Sr. is said to have instructed some seamen to blow up houses in the path of the fire, thus creating a break and saving the church. Strangely enough, the same story is told by a warden at nearby St. Olave's church in Hart Street, but this time the hero was Samuel Pepys, who was trying to save his own parish church. In either case both men lived in the area and would have been concerned about

8

their homes and their churches.

The church also has one other non-theatrical American association. John Quincy Adams was married here in 1797. Its present theatrical connections stem from its use by the annual City of London Festival every July as a performance venue for dramatic recitals, which are usually well worth catching if your visit coincides.

*Leave All Hallows by the same door you entered. Directly across from you is the entrance to* **Seething Lane**. *Take the subway back to the opposite side of the street. One block up Seething Lane is a small park called appropriately* **Seething Lane Gardens**. *At its center is a pleasant*

St. Olave's Hart Street

**8**

bust of the neighborhood's most famous resident—Samuel Pepys. *A little farther on, again on the right, is* **Pepys Street**, *where the great 17th century diarist lived for many years.* We should perhaps say a bit about this man, whose name occurs almost as often as Shakespeare's in these walks. Pepys, who lived from 1633 to 1703, spent most of his adult life as an administrator in the British naval service, and in the course of his duties achieved an extraordinarily wide background of travel, knowledge, and social contacts. He was, among other things, an avid theatre-goer, and his extensive diaries remain one of the best sources for firsthand information about the Restoration theatre in particular and life in 17th century England in general.

*On your left now you will see* **St. Olave's Hart Street**, *another fine old church that had to be almost completely rebuilt after destruction by German bombs. Enter the churchyard beneath a macabre gateway of skulls with its Latin motto, "Mors mihi lucrum", which translates as "Death is a light to me."* Dickens in *The Uncommercial Traveller* referred to it as his "best beloved churchyard St. Ghastly Grim." *If the yard is not open, proceed to the next corner and turn left to find the other door to the church. Inside the church, notice in particular the*

**The Ship**

memorial to Samuel Pepys in the right aisle. Look also at the bust set in a niche high on the left beyond the pulpit. It is Pepys' wife Elizabeth, who died at the age of twenty-nine, and seems to be positioned so that he could look at her as he sat in his pew. Both husband and wife are reunited now in the crypt beneath the altar. Lunchtime concerts take place here on some Wednesdays and Thursdays.

Leave the church through the exit opposite the churchyard and you will find yourself on **Hart Street**. To your left a splash of color and a pub sign of a clipper ship in full sail should catch your eye. It is the front of an Art nouveau Pub called the **Ship**, dating from the 1890s. It must be one of the most fanciful tavern fronts in the city. Don't bother to go in, as the interior has been remodeled into nondescript brewery modern.

After a glance at the pub front retrace your steps back past the church and down what is now called **Crutched Friars** toward the bleak stone arch of **Fenchurch Station**. This unusual street name comes from the

13th century friary of the Holy Cross that stood in Hart Street. The monks wore a cross as their emblem and were known as the "crossed" or "crutched" order.

Once under the arch of Fenchurch station, take a peek at the pub called The Cheshire Cheese. This is not the famous one, which is just off Fleet street (See Walk 5), but it is enchanting in a musty sort of way, with its decor of old Victorian prints and stuffed animal heads.

**Crutched Friars**

**8**

*Continue straight on Crutched Friars, which finally turns into **Jewry Street** and shortly intersects with **Aldgate**, site of another one of the four original gates into the city.* Geoffrey Chaucer occupied apartments above this gate from 1374 to 1385. *Cross the busy intersection toward **St. Bodolph Aldgate**, by George Dance the elder.* If the crowd about the church looks a bit seedy, don't be worried. A ministry located in the crypt offers shelter and food to the indigent.

*Our route takes us along the west side of the church (i.e. the church is on your right) and up **Houndsditch**, which is the street dead ahead of you. This is a maddening intersection. Unless you are insane enough to vault the metal barriers, you will have to work your way over to Houndsditch via a subway (that's an underpass, remember). There's one on the corner labeled Exit 7. If you miss that one there's another labeled Exit 5 around the corner in back of the church. No matter which one you enter make sure you leave by Exit 3. When you emerge just keep walking straight ahead on Houndsditch. There should be a **post office** on your right.*

*With a bit of imagination, if you have any left after negotiating that intersection, you can see yourself now walking on Houndsditch parallel to the old city wall that ran from Aldgate to Bishopgate. Your feet are treading on the moat or ditch constructed outside the walls for additional safety. The name apparently comes from some well-known 12th century kennels for hunting dogs that were located just outside the walls of the city. Even before you get to the corner you will see the spire of **St. Bodolph Without Bishopsgate**. That should happen about the same time*

**8**

**St. Bodolph Without Bishopsgate**

*you pass a pub called The Drum and Monkey.*

    *Houndsditch ends at **Bishopsgate**, which stood until 1760 at a point to your left as you reach the intersection. The church of course is a bit to your right as it stood "without" Bishopsgate.* The elder George Dance had a hand in the design of this church as well as the one back at Aldgate. Our theatrical connection is that we are now in Alleyn country. In an older St. Bodolf Without Bishopsgate on this site Edward Alleyn (1566-1626), the actor and co-owner/manager of The Fortune Theatre, was baptized. His family home was up Devonshire Row, a small side street to the right off Bishopsgate. An infant son of Ben Jonson was also buried in the old church.

    *If you feel the need for a rest, the churchyard has a pleasant garden and there are lots of sandwich shops in the office complex nearby. Otherwise, turn right immediately onto Bishopsgate and move along past the restored Victorian Gothic pile of the old Great Eastern Hotel. Next is **Liverpool Street Station**, which was originally built in 1874 on the site of the old Bethlehem Hospital for the insane.* This was the original asylum known as Old Bedlam. It gave a word to our language and provides one of the sites of action in the John Webster play, *The Changeling. Directly behind Liverpool street Station is **Broad Street**, which was built on a graveyard where the ill-fated playwright and pamphleteer Robert Greene (1560-1592) was buried.* Greene is today remembered as much for his bitter attack on Shakespeare, ". . . an upstart crow beautified with feathers . . . the only Shakescene in the country," as for his one major dramatic work, *The Honorable History of Friar Bacon and Friar Bungay.*

    *You should now cross through the present day bedlam to the station side of the street, if you haven't already done so. As you go by **Brushfield Street** to your right, you should be able to see the tower of **Christ Church Spitalfields** built by Nicolas Hawksmoor in the early 1700s. This also gives you a vague fix on the once famous **Spitalfields Market**. The area has been scheduled for redevelopment for years. After a fair piece of walking you will arrive at **Primrose Street** where Bishopsgate becomes **Norton Folgate**.* A griffin perched in mid-street marks the end of the City of London. Although the surroundings may be of little help, it should not take too much imagination to see yourself riding or walking out through the old Aldgate, or Moorgate or Bishopsgate on a sunny, spring afternoon in the late 1570s. Your destination might have been the waving flag of a playhouse. If you gaze at any 16th century map of London you will see how the main egress routes flow out past the old city gates and then along familiar strip-mall-like developments into the country. Finsbury Fields, which is where you are, was one such parcel of open space that was decidedly rural yet contiguous to the growing city and the roads that led out of it.

    *Keep walking. When you cross busy **Folgate**, (once Norton Folgate), you have crossed a street on which that short-lived maker of the mighty*

118

line, *Christopher Marlowe, once lived. The next cross street on the left (the sign may be high and to your rear as you reach the curb) is Worship Street, and William Shakespeare is said to have lived there, ("six doors from Norton Folgate").*

*Your next task is to cross the ferocious traffic on the **Great Eastern Road** into the continuation of **Shoreditch High Street**. Two little streets beyond is **Holywell Lane**.* Richard Burbage (1567-1619), the Elizabethan tragic actor, lived near here as did John Webster, author of *The Duchess of Malfi*. Note the narrowness of these lanes even today. The buildings have changed but the basic configuration is still from the 16th century. As we have said, London, like any modern urban area, was growing, ribbon-like, along the main roads out into the countryside. Beyond Holywell Lane, Shoreditch High Street would have been lined with shabby lodging houses, inns, and small businesses. And of course each thoroughfare spawned a network of tiny vein-like side streets.

*Walk on for one more short block, then take the next left turn at the Texaco filling station, into the clearly ancient and narrow course of **New Inn Yard**. Walk on the right hand side of the street. Follow it. Go under the **railroad tracks** and then another block until you strike **Curtain Road**. Don't cross the street; just turn to your right.* A rather neglected looking plaque (just under a purple A. Oakden and Sons Ltd. sign) at 86-88 Curtain Road, marks the approximate site of the first permanent public theatre in England—**The Theatre**. It was constructed in 1576 for about 650 pounds by James Burbage, a carpenter turned actor, and his brother-in-law, John Brayne, a greengrocer. It was set back from the road, was round or polygonal, was made of wood, had a paved yard like an inn, a stage supported by posts, a cover or "heaven" over the stage, a "tiring room" for actors, and "galleries" for spectators. That is what we know about the first permanent commercial theatre building in London even though it functioned for more than twenty years. It is likely that in addition to all of the plays of Shakespeare up to 1597, the best works of the age were displayed here. When this building was dismantled in 1598, the timbers were dragged to Bankside, probably along the route you have just walked, and there re-used to construct a new theatre called The Globe.

**8**

*The site of the second public theatre built in London, The Curtain, is also nearby on the same Holywell Priory land. It is unmarked, but if you wish to visit it, turn back to the south toward the Old Blue Last pub and cross the busy **Great Eastern Street** and pick up **Curtain Road** by a high rise carpark on the other side. On the left-hand side of the road just beyond **Hewlett Street** (and again no doubt back in the field and off the road) was **The Curtain***

THE SITE OF THIS BUILDING FORMS PART OF WHAT WAS ONCE THE PRECINCT OF THE PRIORY OF S. JOHN THE BAPTIST. HOLYWELL WITHIN A FEW YARDS STOOD FROM 1577 TO 1598. THE FIRST LONDON BUILDING SPECIALLY DEVOTED TO THE PERFORMANCE OF PLAYS. AND KNOWN AS "THE THEATRE."

*theatre, cleverly built in 1577 by Henry Laneman in a location just a bit closer to the city gates than The Theatre.* It seemed to have had no predominant company in residence and never had the reputation of The Theatre, though the Lord Chamberlain's Men used the building between 1597 and 1599 before they moved into their new home, The Globe, on Bankside. In later years, when The Curtain was the sole surviving playhouse in Shoreditch, it was used by Queen Anne's and Prince Charles' Men. It was destroyed in 1627.

Little is known of its shape, but Rosemary Linnell has done an excellent job of marshaling the available facts in a tiny 1977 volume titled *The Curtain Playhouse.* Some people have ascribed theatrical significance to the name Curtain Road, but the name Curtain probably refers to an old curtain wall that ran parallel to the original lane.

You have now completed a true journey back into time. You have walked the route that an Elizabethan theatregoer would have taken in order to attend The Theatre or The Curtain. I think it is fair to say that not many 20th century theatrophiles have made this pilgrimage.

*If you have visited the site of The Curtain retrace your steps back to the site of The Theatre and continue on up Curtain Road. You will pass an old building on the left (#83) labeled Burbage House. You are probably the only person in the neighborhood who knows what that refers to. At the first stoplight, which is Old Street, turn right and walk on until the tall, 192 foot spire of **St. Leonard's Shoreditch** appears. That should happen just before you start to walk under a **railway bridge.** Keep walking until you reach the corner across from the church.* The current building, another George Dance the Elder design, dates from 1740, but the older one on this site was the parish church for many of the actors at the Theatre and the Curtain.

*Cross over into the churchyard of St. Leonard's. Don't forget to look for a grisly memento of the parish past in the church grounds. Under a small shed in the north section of the garden are preserved several sets of stocks and an old whipping post.*

*The church is open Monday through Friday and for Sunday services; treat yourself to a view of the large memorial erected in 1913 by the London Shakespeare League.* It is dedicated to the "players, musicians, and other men of the theatre" who were members of the parish or were buried in the church.

Chief amongst these were members of the Burbage family. James Burbage (1530-1597), actor, entrepreneur, and builder of The Theatre is buried here, as is his elder son Cuthbert, the manager and builder of the Globe, and his younger son Richard (1567-1619), the great tragedian. They all lived and worked in the Shoreditch area.

Richard Burbage began his career in 1585 with the Admiral's Men. Around 1588 he joined Lord Strange's Men and probably made the acquaintance of a young actor and budding playwright named William

Shakespeare. By 1598 both men were shareholders in the Chamberlain's Men. Burbage would, in the next few years, create, among others, the roles of Hamlet, King Lear, Othello, and Richard III. When he was buried at old St. Leonard's in March of 1619, "people flocked from all parts of London, in honour of the first sovereign of the English stage."

In addition to the Burbage dynasty, the church memorial also pays homage to a number of other local players. There is William Somer (?-1560), a court jester for Henry VIII, and Mr. Richard Tarleton (?-1588) the foremost comic actor of the Elizabethan Period. Tarleton was best known for his performances of Elizabethan jigs (medleys of rhymes and songs that were sung and danced to the tunes of popular melodies). Like many gifted comedians, he was an inveterate improviser, and the *Oxford Companion to the Theatre* suggests that Shakespeare had Tarleton in mind when he referred to poor Yorick, the King's jester, in *Hamlet*. He may also have been thinking of him when he has Hamlet, in his speech to the players, say, "Let those that play your clowns speak no more than is set down for them." But his natural gifts are thought to have inspired Shakespeare to create such popular comic parts as Launce, Bottom and Dogberry; a drawing of him may be found preserved in a manuscript at the British Museum.

In 1598 Mr. Gabriel Spencer, a player at the Rose Theatre on Bankside, was buried here. He was not a parish resident but was dispatched during a duel at Hoxton Fields, which was just to the north. His killer was none other than the playwright Ben Jonson.

Also honored are William Sly (?-1608), another principal actor in Shakespeare's company, and Richard Cowley, a bit part player. A final theatrical burial, just before the old church was destroyed, was that of George Lillo (1693-1739), best remembered as the author of *The London Merchant; or, the History of George Barnwell*. The play was immensely popular both in London and on the continent. It has come to be known as one of the early examples of middle class sentimental tragedy.

**8**

*At this point the walk is done. You have two main transportation options. From the front of the church you can get on a bus and return to the West End. The Number 6 or 22 will take you all the way to Piccadilly and beyond or you can simply ride down to Liverpool St. Station and connect with the tube there. If you still have some snap in your step and feel totally committed to the Underground, you can walk back down Old Street to the Old Street tube station. This is, however, a good seven or eight blocks. Walk 9 does start at the Old Street station and will deposit you at the Barbican Center (London home of the Royal Shakespeare Company for half the year) in fairly short order.*

*If you have more time on your hands and are interested in period furniture or design, it is about six blocks up Kingsland Road to the Geffrye Museum [a bus is available], where a series of period rooms is* *arranged in chronological order. Also in this part of the city is the Bethnal Green Museum of Childhood. It features toys, dollhouses, and model soldiers. To get there, return down **Shoreditch High Street** to **Bethnal Green Road** and from there take an 8 or 8a bus east to the Cambridge Heath Road. [See a standard museum guide for more detailed descriptions of these museums.]*

**8**

# WALK NINE

# DOING BATTLE
# AROUND THE
# BARBICAN

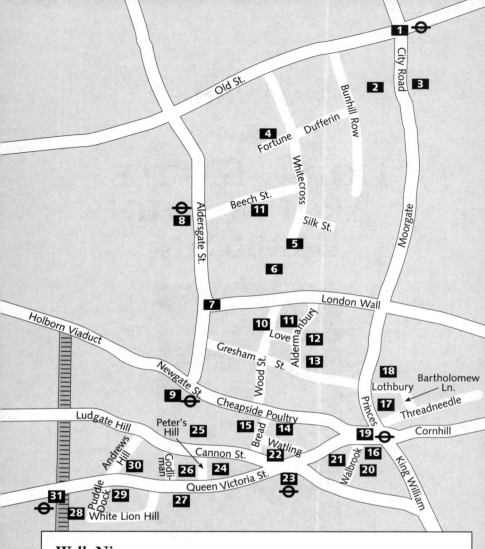

## Walk Nine

1. Old Street Tube station
2. Bunhill Fields Cemetery
3. Wesley Chapel
4. Fortune Theatre site
5. Barbican Centre
6. St. Giles Without Cripplegale
7. Museum of London
8. Barbican Tube Station
9. St. Paul's Tube Station
10. Church of St. Albans
11. Site of Wren Church of St. Mary Aldermanbury

12. Guildhall
13. St. Lawrence Jewry
14. St. Mary-Le-Bow
15. Mermaid Tavern site
16. Mansion House
17. Bank of England
18. St. Margaret, Lothbury
19. Bank Tube Station
20. Church of St. Stephen Walbrook
21. Temple of Mithras remains
22. Church of St. Mary Aldermary

23. Mansion House Tube Station
24. St. Nicholas Cole Abbey
25. St. Paul's Cathedral
26. College of Arms
27. St. Benet
28. Blackfriars
29. Mermaid Theatre
30. Church of St. Andrew by the Wardrobe
31. Blackfriars Tube Station

⊖ Tube Station

**STARTING POINT:** Old Street Station (Northern Line)

**APPROXIMATE TIME:** The better part of a day if you do all three parts.

P*art I of this walk takes you to a fascinating cemetery, the site of the Fortune Theatre, a lively street
market, and finally on to the home of England's
Royal Shakespeare Company at the Barbican. (Since 1996
the RSC has decided only to occupy the Barbican for six
months of the year, and to tour the country for the other six
months.) The walking part of this section can be polished off
easily in forty-five minutes. If you are planning a full day,
you might begin between 10:00 or 11:00 AM. This will get
you to the Barbican complex in time to check for facility tours,
order some RSC tickets, and have a leisurely lunch on the
patio. If you are on a tight budget and the weather is pleasant, grab a sandwich and drink at the tube station and have
a picnic at the little park in Bunhill Fields.*

*Part II takes you to St. Giles Church and the Museum of
London. [Note: the museum is closed on Mondays.] Even with
a stop at the church, the walk to the Museum of London won't
take more than twenty minutes. The museum visit could be
lengthy. I usually have difficulty getting out of the bookstore
in less than an hour.*

*Part III visits several Wren churches, the Guildhall, a
Roman Temple, some Shakespeare sites, and the Mermaid
Theatre. This part involves a fair hike and could be sched-
uled separately if you spend a lot of time in the museum.
There are several tube stops along the route so it can be trun-
cated if you get tired or the hour gets too late.*

## Part I
### *(Less than an hour)*

O*ur starting point is the* **Old Street Tube Station** *(Northern Line).
Take Exit 5 out of the station. Walk straight ahead down* **City Road**
*as you emerge. You'll shortly pass an office block called Monmouth House*

9

**Bunhill Fields Cemetary**

*if you're on the right track. Keep a sharp eye out for the welcome greenery of the* **Bunhill Fields Cemetery.**

*Just before you reach the cemetery, there is an interesting diversion to your left. The* **Wesley Chapel,** *mother church of world Methodism, and John Wesley's home, now a museum, are available for inspection should you so choose. Otherwise turn right into the Bunhill Fields Cemetery opposite. The name is thought to be a corruption of bonehill after the piles of bones that would be exposed as the burial ground was reused in successive generations.* The cemetery is also unusual because its position, outside of the old city walls, allowed it to accept Jews and other "nonconformists" for burial. *The walk through the cemetery is now fenced in to keep you out of the burial grounds proper, but several of the important markers have been moved to the open area at the center of the cemetery. On your left at the main path crossing is the grave of John Bunyan (1628-88) author of* A Pilgrim's Progress. *On your right is the obelisk for the novelist, Daniel Defoe (1660-1731) and next to it the stone of poet and engraver William Blake (1757-1827). A bit further to the right is a pleasant little pocket park with clean public loos. Picnic here if you purchased some food at the tube station.*

As you enter Bunhill Fields the city recedes and birdsong takes over. London is not really buildings and traffic; it is history and people. Here in Bunhill Fields the "silent majority" reasserts its power. The stones—chipped, flaking, broken, stained with age, dappled with moss—are eloquent in their silence. They march in measured rows like ghostly grey soldiers over a green carpet. William Blake rests easily here. Mortality and faith repose in quiet equilibrium.

If you are interested in more details of the cemetery, a booklet used to be available at the park keeper's kiosk.

*Return from the little park to the crossing at the middle of the cemetery and turn right down the path between the graves. You will ultimately emerge from the cemetery onto* **Bunhill Row**. *Take a few steps to the left on this street and then go right on* **Dufferin Street**. *In about two blocks Dufferin Street reaches* **Whitecross Street**. *If you arrive before 2:30 or 3:00 in the afternoon, the intersection marks the bottom end of an extremely colorful local street market. Make a right turn and check out the wares for a bit.*

*When you are ready to leave, return to the intersection where you started. To your right Dufferin Street becomes Fortune Street. Make that turn and keep your eyes a little above head height to the right. You will see a blue plaque marking the approximate site of what some might say was the second most famous Elizabethan theatre—the Fortune.* It was built in 1600 for Richard Henslowe and Edward Alleyn by Peter Streete, a carpenter who had recently done a similar job on Bankside's Globe Theatre for the Burbage brothers. The building contract for The Fortune survives in Henslowe's papers, but at several key junctures the contract unfortunately tells Mr. Streete to simply follow the model of The Globe. Once again that nagging question surfaces, "What did the interior of an Elizabethan theatre really look like?" Interestingly, however, some of the measurements that do occur in the Fortune contract have been used in working out the dimensions for the current Bankside Globe reconstruction.

*Step back now to the intersection and turn right.* Think of this busy corner as the nexus of a conduit that fed people out of the city through Cripplegate or Moorgate into the more open spaces of the Finsbury Fields area. Henslowe and Alleyn were not fools when it came to business. Small villages were growing and suburbs were springing up in the area. Travel all the way through the city and across the river to reach Bankside was less than convenient. And out here they would

**9**

not have to compete directly with their chief rivals, The Chamberlain's Men, with their sumptuous new Globe and their well-known and respected playwright William Shakespeare.

*Continue walking now away from the*

**Fortune Theatre site**

street market. *On the left are more markets, a covered mall, and a large Safeway food store. Ahead of you rise the mirrored skins and brutal towers of the Barbican Estate. If you want a brief respite and a chance to see the Barbican towers more clearly, turn right into Shrewsbury Court just past the pub on the corner. You'll find a nice little playground, some green space, and several benches. If you take this diversion turn right again when you return to Whitecross Street. A brief walk on down Whitecross and across busy* **Beech Street** *into Silk Street will take you to the main* **Barbican Centre entrance.**

*As you move down the curved drive you will see the Royal Shakespeare Theatre's stage door on your left. Just beyond is an enclosed rectangle about 12 by 50 feet in size. This is the lift used to deliver scenery to the RSC scene docks. A fully loaded lorry drives on and then is lowered down into the bowels of the building. If you are lucky enough to find the lift down, it is quite a sight. You peer over the railings and wonder just what a truck is doing down there in a hole that appears to have no exit.*

*Just past the lift is the main entrance. An information desk and the main ticket office for the centre is located to your right. You can book tickets for any event right here. When the RSC is away on tour other national and international companies may be seen here.*

The building as a whole contains in addition to two theatres, a concert hall, an excellent public library with a fine theatre and general arts collection, restaurants at all price ranges, a cinema, art galleries, exhibition halls, conference rooms, book stalls, and special facilities for the Guildhall School of Music and Drama.

# Part II
*(20 to 30 minutes)*

St. Giles Without Cripplegate

*With a tour and lunch out of the way, pick up your walk again at the church of **St. Giles Without Cripplegate.** You can see your destination clearly from the Lakeside Terrace on the Ground Floor. To reach the church take the stairs or lift up to Level 2, turn right, go out through the heavy doors and past a security station. Then turn right again onto Gilbert Bridge, which is the causeway across the lake. At the far side you will find some stairs that will descend back into St. Giles Square.*

The ancient church that sits on St. Giles Square is the only building in the 600 acre Barbican site that pre-dates World War II. The main fabric, much restored after the World War II bombing that leveled the surrounding area, dates from 1545. John Bunyan and Daniel Defoe, whose graves you passed a short time ago in Bunhill Fields Cemetery, were worshippers here. So were Sir Thomas More, and the musician, Thomas Morley. Edward Alleyn, co-owner of the nearby Fortune Theatre, is also said to have attended services here. Oliver Cromwell, the Great Protector, was married here, as was Ben Jonson.

The most famous grave in the church is that of the poet John Milton, whose gravestone is set in the floor at the alter rail, facing the east window. A lifesize statue of him gazes at you from the north aisle. Several members of the family of Sir Thomas Lucy are also buried here. Lucy, you may remember, was the landowner and magistrate of Stratford who supposedly caught and punished the young Shakespeare for poaching and literally helped drive the boy out of Stratford and to his better fortunes. Justice Shallow in *The Merry Wives of Windsor* is felt by some to be a satirical portrait of Sir Thomas.

*Several historical display boards provide a fascinating history of the church. Upon leaving the church walk around the building to your left*

**9**

129

*where you will find a pleasant paved terrace overlooking a pond and a splendidly preserved section of the medieval London Wall. Continue around the church until you are back at the stairway where you entered the square. On your left is a pub called Crowder's Well, opposite the City of London School for Girls.*

*To head for the **Museum of London**, climb back up the stairs and turn right at the top, away from the Barbican complex. Take another right at the next passage labeled Wallside. From now on it's as if you were patrolling the parapets of the great wall around the city of London itself. Each step gives you another striking view of St. Giles and the Barbican estate. Continue to follow the yellow brick line on the floor. Go past Thomas More House. Watch for a left turn into a covered passage called the John Wesley Highwalk and a sign saying "Museum." This walkway will wind and twist onto the Thomas More Highwalk, but will ultimately deposit you at the entrance to the Museum of London, which was built just outside the old city walls and on the site of another old Jewish Cemetery.*

This magnificently arranged museum is one of London's better bargains. You could easily spend the rest of the day here. There are several theatrical exhibits including a new one on the excavations at the Rose Theatre site. The bookstore is also superlative. Try not to rush this visit. The museum is closed Mondays (except Bank Holidays), open Tuesday through Saturday 10 to 5:50, Sundays 12 to 5:50. *If the time gets away from you, just call it a day and ask for directions to the **Barbican** or **St. Paul's Tube station**.*

**9**

**London Wall**

# Part III
### *(1½ to 2 hours)*

**W**hen you leave the museum, take a left onto the walkway marked *Nettleton Court, which shortly turns into Bastion High Walk. More of the ancient city walls (the same ones you saw from inside the museum) will shortly appear on your left. Stop at the explanatory plaque. The street below and to the right is London Wall and somewhere between here and the next street ahead (**Wood Street**) was the now vanished Silver Street.*

In late 1603 or early 1604 William Shakespeare moved into the home of Christopher Mountjoy, which was located on Silver Street near Cripplegate. It was a prudent move for several reasons. This was a far more fashionable district than Bankside, Will's fellow players and friends Heminge and Condell lived nearby, and it would be easy to slip out on an afternoon and check out the competition at The Fortune.

Mountjoy was a French Huguenot who made headdresses and ornaments for women. He also had a daughter who fell in love with one of his apprentices, a young man by the name of Stephen Belott. Shakespeare was apparently asked to assist in arranging the marriage. The details of the affair came to light in 1612 when Will was asked to give a deposition in a court case in which the now estranged young Belott was suing old Charles Mountjoy for non-payment of some promised parts of his daughter's dowry. This deposition, which was taken in Stratford, gives us our only clue to Shakespeare's everyday speech habits and also provides us with one of his six surviving signatures.

*Walk on now toward the hovering presence of a huge new office block called Alban Court. In order to take advantage of air rights the building was built over the intersection of Wood street, and it is a remarkable piece of engineering, like a massive erector set. Turn right as you reach a covered courtlike area at the end of Bastion High Walk. If you stand at the end of this terrace you can look down Wood Street at the solitary steeple fragment of the church of St. Albans—a World War II bombing victim that was never rebuilt. But it's now time to get back to street level. There's an escalator to your right or a ramp to your left. Either one will suffice. Once you have reached Wood Street walk past the remnant of St. Albans and turn left almost immediately into **Love Lane**, behind the steeple.*

*In a short block you will see on your left a tiny open plot of green. This space preserves the foundation stones of the Wren **church of St. Mary Aldermanbury**.* The bombed ruins of this church were labeled stone by stone and transported to the United States where, reconstructed, they stand today in Fulton, Missouri. It was at the dedication of the reassembled church that Sir Winston Churchill made his famous speech in which the term "Iron Curtain" was coined and where not too long ago former Soviet Premier Gorbachev officially declared that the cold

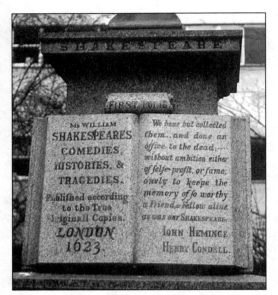

war was over. *We stop here, though, because the little square also contains a monument surmounted by a bust of William Shakespeare.*

Ironically, the memorial isn't for Will but for his fellow players and friends John Heminge and William Condell, who were church wardens of and buried in St. Mary Aldermanbury. Heminge (1556-1630) was a member of Lord Strange's Men for a time, a member of the Chamberlain's Men, and may have been the first actor to play Falstaff. Although he appears to have retired from acting about 1611, he con-

**Monument to Heminge & Condell, publishers of the first folio edition of Shakespeare**

tinued on as business manager of the company. He is mentioned in Shakespeare's will and was a trustee in the Blackfriars gatehouse purchase. Like Shakespeare, he appears to have ended his days a well fixed and comfortable burgher.

Condell (?-1627) seems to have joined the Chamberlain's Men about 1594 at the same time Shakespeare did, but did not become a shareholder until 1612. In 1623 Heminge and Condell gave the plays of William Shakespeare to the ages by compiling and overseeing the publication of the First Folio edition of his works. Without this labor of love many of the plays might have been lost forever. No truer friends had any man in terms of what they gave of their colleague to the rest of the world.

*Follow Shakespeare's gaze out of the churchyard and walk west down* **Aldermanbury***. A left turn just past the new Guildhall Library, which contains a nice bookstore and exhibit area, will put you into the square in front of the* **Guildhall***. The Guildhall is the ceremonial seat of government for the City of London. You may wish to visit the medieval crypt or the Great Hall. The entrance is to your left. Descriptions are available inside but one thing they may not tell you is this theatrical tidbit. The inscription on the monument to Lord Nelson in the Great Hall was composed by the dramatist Richard Brinsley Sheridan. The Guildhall is open 10 to 5 Monday through Saturday all year round, except when required for a grand State occasion, and in the summer months on Sunday as well.*

*Directly in front of the Guildhall and across the courtyard is the Wren church of St. Lawrence Jewry. Look at the weather vane atop the spire.*

9

*It is shaped like the grid iron on which St. Lawrence was roasted alive. A visit is possible if you wish; if not as you pass note that the Jacobean dramatist Thomas Middleton was baptized in the pre-Wren church and that Sir Thomas More preached there.*

*As you exit the Guildhall Yard, you will almost immediately be out on* **Gresham Street.** *Turn right on Gresham and proceed one block until you meet up with* **Wood Street** *once again. Turn left on Wood Street until the tee junction at* **Cheapside.** *To your left you get a gorgeous view of the 222-foot spire of* **St. Mary-Le-Bow.** To be a true Cockney (or Londoner) you must have been born within the sound of the Bow bells that supposedly recalled the apprentice Dick Whittington to his hard duties in the city of London. The crypt of strong Norman arches (the first in the city built on "bows" of stones) still exists, although the church has been much changed inside. The spire is one of Christopher Wren's finest and prompted an admirer

St. Mary-Le-Bow

**9**

to say in 1750 that "the steeple of Bow Church is as perfect as human imagination can contrive."

*Now cross the street, jog ten yards to the left and enter **Bread Street**. A house or two from the corner, on your right about where the fountain is in the subterranean court, stood the famous **Mermaid Tavern** where Ben Jonson held sway the first Friday of every month.* William Shakespeare was also a regular, for Jonson wrote in reference to him, "That such thy drought was and so great thy thirst, that all thy plays were drawn at the Mermaid first."

A man by the name of Fuller in 1662 recalled Jonson and Shakespeare in witty combat at the inn and described it thus:

> Master Jonson (like a Spanish galleon)
> built for higher in learning, solid but
> slow in his performance. Shakespeare,
> with the English man of war, lesser in
> bulk, but lighter in sailing . . . could
> take advantage of all winds by the
> quickness of his wit and invention.

Among the other wits, artists, and poets who frequented the Mermaid were Christopher Marlowe, Michael Drayton, John Donne, Inigo Jones, Thomas Campion, Beaumont and Fletcher, Sir Walter Raleigh, and much later on, in the 19th century, the poet John Keats, who cemented its fame with the lines:

> Souls of poets dead and gone,
> What Elysium have you known,
> Happy field or mossy cavern,
> Choicer than the Mermaid Tavern.

*Return to **Cheapside** and turn right. Pass St. Mary-Le-Bow and visit the wonderfully light and airy interior. Cross to the other side of the street after you leave or pass the church and continue on eastward on Cheapside (a corruption of the word cheap or market) until it turns into **Poultry** (which was the old chicken market) and finally reaches the confusing and muddled Bank intersection that represents the true center of the City of London. **The Mansion House** (home of the Lord Mayor of London) is on your right. A bit ahead and on your left, occupying the space between **Princes Street** and **Threadneedle Street**, is the impressive and austere facade of Sir John Soane's most famous building, the **Bank of England**.* Actually only the windowless perimeter is Soane's work; the seven-story interior is a 1925-39 rebuilding. The dramatist Richard Brinsley Sheridan once called the bank "The Old Lady of Threadneedle Street." A cartoonist picked up on it and the name has stuck ever since.

*Turn to your left up **Princes Street** and then right on **Lothbury** where Restoration theatre owner Thomas Killigrew was born. About one-third of the way down the block you will see on your left the spire of **St. Margaret, Lothbury**.* This church is built right over one of the lost rivers of London (The Walbrook), which curves to run right under the Bank of England as well. The church escaped World War II destruction and the intimate interior is a Wren original, not a reconstruction. The furnishings come from several other now gone or destroyed churches and include a font and pulpit by Grinling Gibbons and a magnificent carved screen that features two-strand open work balusters that are truly a marvel of grace and skill. *When you leave the church, turn left and then right on* **Bartholomew Lane.** *Turn right again on Threadneedle Street and you will shortly be back at the busy Bank corner once again. Now you can brag that you have been all around the Bank of England.*

*Now look for a* **tube station** *access sign and head downstairs. Once under the intersection, find an exit sign marked Queen Victoria Street/Walbrook. Emerge on* **Walbrook.** *You are still in the bed of the stream that has come out from under the Bank of England and will now flow South down to the Thames. A short distance down Walbrook on your left at the corner of Bucklersbury is the Wren Church of St. Stephen Walbrook.* It is an odd building set on an oddly cramped site. The square tower is topped by a spire that seems a bit too small, but the interior is set around a remarkable dome, that is said to be an experiment for the later St. Paul's. Some people feel it is more beautiful than St. Paul's. Our theatre quest can also be satisfied here since the church is the last resting place of the architect and author Sir John Vanbrugh. Although perhaps best known as the architect of the great palace of the Dukes of Marlborough at Blenheim, Vanbrugh also designed the Queen's Theatre in the Haymarket (1705) and wrote several witty 18th century comedies including *The Relapse* (1696) and *The Provok'd Wife* (1697), both of which are still frequently revived on the English stage. After years of restoration, the church has now reopened on Monday through Thursday from 10 to 4, and Fridays 10 to3. It is closed weekends.

*To the right and away from the church is Bucklersbury Street. Walk the short block down to* **Queen Victoria Street,** *then bend left and keep a sharp eye out for the* **remains of the Temple of Mithras,** *a Roman House of Worship, found during foundation excavations for the large building behind in 1954. It has been moved to its present location in front of Temple Court.*

*Proceeding on down Queen Victoria Street you will arrive at another major street intersection. On the right, in the pie shaped piece bounded by Queen Victoria Street and* **Watling Street,** *is the Wren* **church of St. Mary Aldermary.** *It has a delightful ceiling of most un-Wren-like fan vaulting. It is open Thursdays and Fridays from 11 to 3.*

*Continue the stroll down Queen Victoria Street. If the hour is getting late or your feet are giving out, you may truncate the walk at the* **Mansion House Tube Station.**

*If you wish to continue, forge on past the tube station on Queen Victoria Street toward* **Friday Street** *where you will see on your right*

**9**

the first church that Christopher Wren put his efforts to after the Great Fire of London. **St. Nicholas Cole Abbey** *(1667) is dramatically interesting because of its late 19th century rector, Henry Clay Shuttleworth. Shuttleworth, who spoke out eloquently and at length on labor and housing conditions in late Victorian England, was one of George Bernard Shaw's models for the socialist vicar, James Mavor Morrell in* Candida.

*A little farther on, again on your right, is the well known Peter's Hill view of **St. Paul's Cathedral**. This is followed shortly by the* **College of Arms.** William Shakespeare would have dealt with them when he was pursuing the granting of a Coat of Arms for his father in 1596. *Just across from the College, on your left now, is another Wren church. This elegant little*

St. Nicholas Cole Abbey

*jewel, called **St. Benet,** has now been boxed in by modern sterile brick on two sides and a raised motorway on a third*. It lies nestled, forlorn, and generally overlooked by most people who pass by. The old church would have been visible from the Globe Theatre located just across the Thames and may have prompted the line in *Twelfth Night* Act V Scene 1 when the clown says, " . . . the triplex sir is a good tripping measure; or the bells of St. Benet, sir, may put you in mind: one, two, three."

As rebuilt by Wren, St. Benet has rich red and blue brick, striking white corner dressings, and large airy windows. Inigo Jones—the stage designer, architect, and father of English Class-

**9**

St. Benet

**Peter's Hill view of
St. Paul's Cathedral**

icism—was laid to rest in the old church in 1652 a scant twelve years before the Great Fire of London destroyed the building. Novelist Henry Fielding (1707-1754) was married in the present building. For theatrical trivia buffs the church also contains the tomb of John Charles Brooke, an officer of the College of Arms, who was one of the six-teen people crushed to death when George III and his queen caused a riot during a visit to the Haymarket Theatre in 1794.

*In order to continue now you must take the subway under White Lion Hill. Follow a sign that points you toward **Blackfriars** and the **Mermaid Theatre**. Once back at street level you will see shortly on your right the church of **St. Andrew by the Wardrobe**. We looked at the other side of this church on Walk Two. You may also remember that just up St. Andrew's Hill was the Blackfriars Priory Gatehouse purchased by William Shakespeare in 1613.* (It is uncertain as to whether Shakespeare ever actually lived there, but it was a stone's throw from the Blackfriars Theatre, which was the winter home of The Chamberlain's Men.)

*At the next stoplighted intersection a slight bend to the left will take you to **Puddle Dock** and **The Mermaid Theatre**.* When it was opened on May 29, 1959 the bells of St. Paul's pealed a welcome to the first new theatre to be built within the confines of the City of London since the Puritans closed down the theatres in the 1640s. It was as

9

137

much the brainchild of Bernard Miles (later Lord Miles) as the reconstructed Globe Theatre was of Sam Wanamaker. Miles persuaded the City of London companies to put up the money, and ran some very adventurous and successful seasons, with a repertoire that included revivals of infrequently-seen classics: John Ford's *'Tis Pity She's a Whore*; little-known works by the famous: Sean O'Casey's *The Bishop's Bonfire;* and unusual new plays—an adaptation of Frederick Rolfe's novel, *Hadrian VII.*

The Mermaid has been re-constructed recently, but was originally built within the shell of a bombed out Thameside warehouse. It had an open proscenium stage, with seating for around five hundred people in one sharply rising bank. At its opening, Caroline Hawkins, the four-year-old daughter of actor Jack Hawkins, was rowed up the Thames dressed as a mermaid. She was carried into the theatre and presented on stage to the Lord Mayor of London, who took off her tail to symbolize that the Mermaid was here to stay. That remains to be seen, as the still quite unfashionable location has caused the theatre to be dark a great deal in the past several years, since the departure of Bernard Miles.

*With that fish story you may not to wish to stay around any longer either. There's not much to see at the theatre and the **Blackfriars tube station** is just a few steps away across the intersection in front of you.*

9

# THE NOT SO BRIGHT LIGHTS OF SOHO

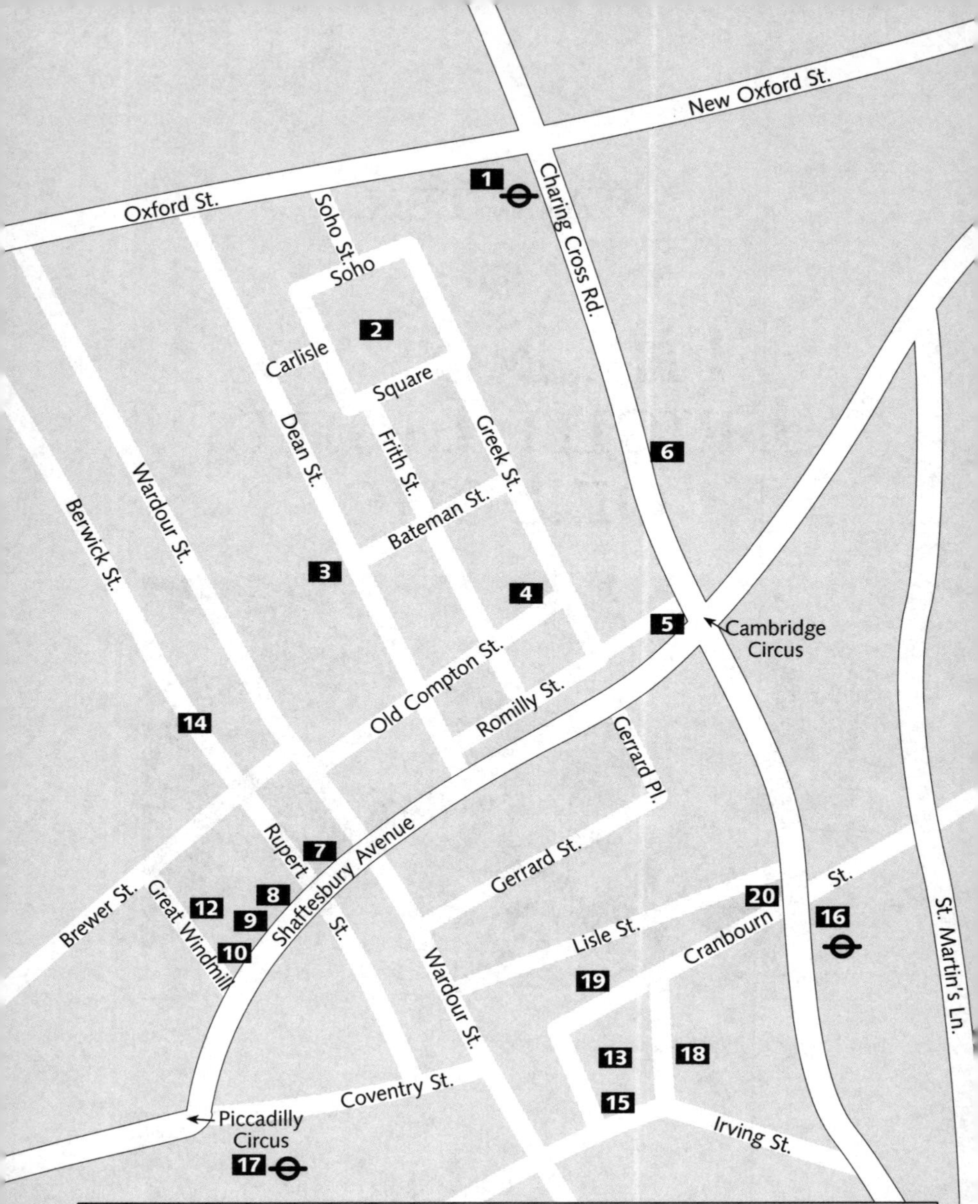

New Oxford St.

Oxford St.

Soho St.

Soho

Carlisle

Square

Dean St.

Frith St.

Greek St.

Bateman St.

Charing Cross Rd.

**1** ⊖

**2**

**6**

**3**

**4**

**5** ← Cambridge Circus

Old Compton St.

Romilly St.

Gerrard Pl.

**14**

Rupert

Shaftesbury Avenue

**7**

Berwick St.

Wardour St.

Great Windmill

**12** **8**
**9**
**10**

St.

Brewer St.

Gerrard St.

Lisle St.

Cranbourn

St.

St. Martin's Ln.

**20**

**16** ⊖

**19**

Wardour St.

**13** **18**

**15**

Coventry St.

Irving St.

← Piccadilly Circus

**17** ⊖

## Walk Ten

1 Tottenham Ct. Tube Station
2 Soho Square
3 Royalty Theatre site
4 Prince Edward Theatre
5 Palace Theatre
6 Phoenix Theatre
7 Queen's Theatre
8 Gielgud Theatre

9 Apollo Theatre
10 Lyric Theatre
11 Trocadero
12 Windmill Theatre site
13 Leicester Square
14 Berwick St. Market
15 Half Price Ticket Booth
16 Leicester Square Tube Station

17 Piccadilly Circus Tube Station
18 Odeon Cinema
19 Empire Cinema & Dance Hall
20 London Theatre site
⊖ Tube Station

**STARTING POINT:** Tottenham Court Road Tube Station (Central and Northern Line).

**APPROXIMATE TIME:** One to one and one-quarter hours without a lunch stop.

T*his walk covers some important theatres of the past, introduces you to several current West End theatres, and deposits you in Leicester Square at the half price theatre ticket booth. Time your start to get you to the square at least 30 minutes before its scheduled opening, normally 1:00 PM. If it's a nice day consider packing a lunch to eat in Soho Square.*

L*eave the* **Tottenham Court Road Tube Station** *through the exit labeled* **Oxford Street** *South Side. There's a McDonalds dead ahead of you as you reach the street. Once topside, turn left and walk down to* **Soho Street** *(the first traffic signal), where you turn left again.*

*Walk down Soho Street. It is a short block to pleasant, tree shaded* **Soho Square.** *If you're here around lunchtime on a nice day this park will be overflowing with office workers taking their lunch and some of those rare English rays of sunshine. Find yourself a bench or plot of grass left or right of the entrance and sit a spell or have your lunch while you read the next few paragraphs.*

According to Arthur Mee in his classic *London: The City and Westminster,* the name Soho comes from the hunting cry "So-ho" which was used by Charles II's illegitimate son, the unfortunate Duke of Monmouth, an early resident of the district, to try and rally his beleaguered forces against James II at the Battle of Sedgemoor in 1685. The area was farmland in medieval times and belonged to an abbey. In 1536 Henry VIII acquired the land and promptly ceded portions to various supporters. Today's street names such as Monmouth, Leicester, Carlisle, and Newport recall some of those early owners and their palatial homes. Other streets in the area were named after 18th century owners and builders like Wardour, Frith, Gerrard, and Shaftesbury.

The square that surrounds you was laid out in 1681 and has seen a rich dramatic and artistic history. Not enough of the buildings are original to do a walkaround, but the scale remains congenial. As you sit and look about, you should be able to note the statue of Charles II done by Caius Cibber, father of the actor and producer Colley

**10**

141

**Mock Elizabethan hut in Soho Square**

Cibber. On the east or left side of the square as you sit, the actor-manager George Colman the Elder (1732-1794) lived for some eleven years. On the south side, in front of you, was the residence of Charles Kemble. Kemble was a minor actor and manager in a family of considerable renown. His elder brother John Philip Kemble (1757-1823) and his sister Sarah Siddons (1755-1831) were preeminent members of the London theatrical scene. Charles also had an attractive daughter, by the name of Fanny Kemble (1809-93), who lived at number 29 Soho Square with him. She was equally at home in both tragedy and comedy, toured the United States to great acclaim, and lived a varied and interesting life that is well told in a biography titled *Fanny Kemble* by Dorothy Marshall.

On the north side of the square, somewhere behind you, the Soho Academy existed from 1726 to 1805. The school was famous for its Shakespeare performances, and several of its pupils went on to become professional actors.

*You can get up now and stroll toward the center of the square with its little mock Elizabethan hut. At the center turn right and exit the square via **Carlisle Street**. At **Dean Street** turn left.* This is film country now and many production and distribution companies have their offices in the vicinity. Walkers of the world unite and note high on the left on #28 the blue plaque commemorating the former residence of Karl Marx. It is now the Quo Vadis restaurant.

*Another lost London theatre stood at #73 Dean Street (Royalty House), opposite the entrance of Bateman Street. From 1840 to 1953 this was the site of a tiny theatre known as **The Royalty**.* The full story of this remarkable theatre can be read in Mander and Mitchenson's *Lost Theatres of London* and just a brief sample is given here.

**Royalty Theatre site**

The theatre was the brainchild of an actress by the name of Frances Maria Kelly. Miss Kelly had definite ideas about the training of young actors and actresses and decided that she needed her own theatre to do the job right. Her solution was to build her own theatre behind her house at #73 Dean Street. She began her planning for the theatre and accompanying school in 1834, retired from the stage to devote full time to the project in 1835, and completed the theatre in 1840, having sunk most of her wealth into its construction. The opening was disastrous, primarily because of a complicated scene-changing mechanism that had to be operated by a horse-powered treadmill. The chains, blocks, and tackles were so noisy that they made the actors inaudible. When it was operated the entire house shook and, according to one reviewer, gave the audience St. Vitus's Dance.

Miss Kelly finally disappeared from the scene in the mid 1840s, having expended her fortune and her health in the luckless enterprise, but over the next fifty years some of the most important events in the English-speaking theatre occurred in the building. Charles Dickens acted here with his amateur company in Jonson's *Every Man In His Humour* in 1845. In 1875, the initial Gilbert and Sullivan collaboration, *Trial By Jury,* was performed here. Then in 1891, J. T. Grein and his Independent Stage Society took over the theatre and produced the first public performance in England of Henrik Ibsen's *Ghosts.* George Bernard Shaw's first major play *Widower's Houses* was given its initial production here in 1892. That same year also saw the first London production of Brandon Thomas's *Charley's Aunt.* 1893 and 1894 respectively saw the premiers of Ibsen's *A Doll's House* and *The Wild Duck* as well as some of William Poel's experiments in Elizabethan staging. Shaw's *You Never Can Tell* opened there in 1899. There might be a legitimate argument for claiming that the modern theatre in Britain began quite close to where you are now standing.

After the turn of the century the fortunes of the theatre seemed once again hit-and-miss, and it closed down just before World War II. Blitz damage forestalled attempts to re-open after the war and it was finally demolished in 1953 and the present office building, Royalty House, built in 1955. Also laid to rest at that time was the busy ghost of Miss Fanny Kelly, who Joe Mitchenson claims to have seen in 1934.

**10**

*After suitably lamenting the loss of The Royalty, turn to your left down* **Bateman Street** *and travel the short block to the intersection of* **Frith Street.** Up to the left at #64 was the home of the tempestuous actor-manager William Charles Macready (1793-1873). Macready was a notable tragedian, famous for the "the Macready pause," and was one of the few real rivals to Edmund Kean, but is probably better remembered by American theatre buffs because of his keen rivalry with the American actor Edwin Forrest, which led in turn to the Astor Place riot in New York in 1849. That event has been chronicled extensively by theatre historians, but you might want to get a quick popular sense

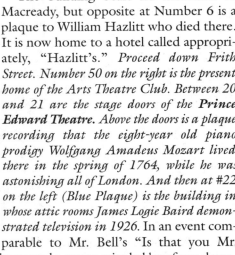

of the affair by reading Richard Nelson's play *Two Shakespearean Actors.*

The building bears no memorial to Macready, but opposite at Number 6 is a plaque to William Hazlitt who died there. It is now home to a hotel called appropriately, "Hazlitt's." *Proceed down Frith Street. Number 50 on the right is the present home of the Arts Theatre Club. Between 20 and 21 are the stage doors of the* **Prince Edward Theatre.** *Above the doors is a plaque recording that the eight-year old piano prodigy Wolfgang Amadeus Mozart lived there in the spring of 1764, while he was astonishing all of London. And then at #22 on the left (Blue Plaque) is the building in whose attic rooms James Logie Baird demon-*

**Hazlitt's**

*strated television in 1926.* In an event comparable to Mr. Bell's "Is that you Mr. Watson," Baird apparently borrowed a young crippled boy from downstairs to sit and become the first human being to appear on a television screen.

*Cross* **Old Compton Street,** *noting the* **Prince Edward Theatre** *on your left.* This theatre was built in the 1930s and spent a lot of time as a cabaret, a restaurant, and a movie theatre until it finally struck it rich with the musical *Evita,* which ran from 1978 to 1986. That was followed by *Chess,* which also had a long run. *Martin Guerre,* the new blockbuster musical by the *Les Miserables* team of Boubil and

Schonberg, opened there in August of 1996 and was extensively rewritten and re-staged in 1997. It was followed by Hal Prince's acclaimed revival of *Showboat* in 1998. *Across the road you may visit the Three Greyhounds, artistic watering hole for many Soho writers and artists who thrive on the cuisine and coviviality of popular publican, Roxy Beaujolais.*

*Shortly now you will reach* **Romilly Street.** *Turn left.* Jean Paul Marat, the French revolutionary, lived on this street in 1776. For theatre buffs the name may be familiar because of the Peter Weiss play of the sixties that won the longest title in the world contest going away. For the record the full title was *The Assassination and Persecution of Jean Paul Marat as Performed by the Inmates of the Asylum of Charenton Under the Direction of the Marquis de Sade.* That's

**Prince Edward Theatre**

*Marat/Sade* for short. *Romilly Street now leads out to the bustle of* **Cambridge Circus** *and the fanciful bulk of the* **Palace Theatre,** *now owned by Sir Andrew Lloyd-Webber.*

This splendidly romantic-looking theatre (its stones red and rich after its recent cleaning) opened its doors in 1891 as the Royal English Opera House. It was renamed the Palace Theatre of Varieties in 1892. Milestone events have included the first appearance of the great ballerina Anna Pavlova in 1910. The theatre was a music hall and revue showcase for several years and then alternated between films and various musical extravaganzas. One of its early long runs was the 655

**10**

**Three Greyhounds**

The Palace
Theatre of
Varieties

performances of the musical *No No Nanette* in 1925 and 1926. Musicals have been the staple since World War II; the 2,385 performance run of *The Sound of Music* from 1961-1967 was followed by Hal Prince's London production of *Cabaret*, starring Judi Dench in her first musical, and Tim Rice and Andrew Lloyd-Webber's *Jesus Christ Superstar*, which opened in 1972. Even that run is just a footnote now as *Les Miserables* started its run in 1986, and a decade and several casts later was still packing them in.

*From the vantage point of the Circus, you can see up **Charing Cross Road** (to your left if you have your back to the Palace) and note another theatre marquee. That's the **Phoenix Theatre** (circa 1930).* The site had previously held a rather low-class music hall called The Alcazar, so the addition of a sleek and sumptuous new legitimate theatre was a boon to the social standing of Upper Charing Cross Road. The current structure opened in 1930 with the premiere production of Noel Coward's *Private Lives*. It featured Coward and Gertrude Lawrence in the leads and a young fellow by the name of Laurence Olivier playing the boorish husband Victor Prynne. As noted by the Olivier biographer, John Cottrell, the future Lord was at the time engaged to be married to actress Jill Esmond and coming off a string of failures. He was not excited by the prospect of playing a simpering supporting role in a piece of nonsense. Coward persuaded him to take the part

10

**The Phoenix Theatre**

by offering him a good salary and an admonition: "Look young man, you'd better be in a success for a change." A success it was, and after three sell-out months in London, Coward transferred it to New York, where the handsome young Olivier caught the eye of Hollywood talent scouts. The climb to fame was on. If you're looking for a good selction of plays, Foyles is nearby in Charing Cross Road.

*Leaving the covered marquee of the Palace, walk down* **Shaftesbury Avenue** *towards* **Piccadilly Circus** *and turn left into* **Gerrard Place**. *Go down one short block and then turn right into* **Gerrard Street** *and you are plumb in the center of London's Chinatown.* While you take in today's oriental flavor, your imagination will have to supply the hall where Thomas Sheridan (1719-88), one of the founders of modern elocution and declamation and the father of playwright and politician Richard Brinsley Sheridan, gave his lectures. *At number 43-44 (on your left) John Dryden (1631-1700) lived and died. A weather-beaten old blue plaque can now just be made out above the Loon Fung*

*supermarket sign. A bit further on at number 35, next to the New Loon Fung restaurant, was the location of another residence of Charles Kemble and his enchanting daughter Fanny.*

*Follow Gerrard Street until you get to **Wardour Street**. Make a left turn there and then at the first turning make another left on **Lisle Street**.* At what was number 9, just before the decaying St. John's Hospital on this rather grubby little backwater, is the house that was the boyhood home of the tempestuous actor Edmund Kean (1787-1833). His uncle, with whom he lived, would buckle a brass collar around the child's neck that read "This boy belongs at number 9 Lisle Street, please bring him home." Kean's early life of deprivation may indeed have given him special insights into the tragic roles that were his forte. He shot to fame in 1814 as Shylock at Drury Lane, and was at his best in villainous and tragic parts, such as Iago, Macbeth and Richard III. A notorious womanizer and heavy drinker, he was once booed as Richard Crookback for being drunk. With typical bravado he roared back at the audience, "If you think I'm drunk, wait till you see Buckingham!" The ultimate compliment was paid by Samuel Taylor Coleridge, who said that "to see him act is like reading Shakespeare by flashes of lightning." The house is now the Hong Kong restaurant.

*Now retrace your steps back to **Wardour Street**, turn right, and walk up to the first traffic signal. This is **Shaftesbury Avenue**. From the corner you can fully appreciate why it is now called the center of London's theatre district—the very heart of the West End. Four legitimate theatres are visible marching in a row down toward Picadilly Circus. They are in order, **The Queen's**, **The Gielgud** (formerly The Globe), **The Apollo**, and **The Lyric**. Turning left at the corner you can stroll down the left side of the street and take in each theatre as you come to it.*

The Queen's Theatre opened in 1907 as a match to The Globe further down the block. World War II bomb damage resulted in the modern facade you see today, but the interior retains its Edwardian flavor. This theatre almost seems to belong to Sir John Gielgud; some of the memorable moments that have graced its stage under his aegis were his great 1930 production of *Hamlet* and the 1937-38 classical season that featured *Richard II*, *The School for Scandal, Three Sisters*, and *The Merchant of Venice*. That quartet of productions had a cast of players that sounds today like a Who's Who of the 20th century theatre. In that company were Peggy Ashcroft, Michael Redgrave, Alec Guinness, Anthony Quayle, George Devine, Glen Byam Shaw, Angela Baddeley, and Rachel Kempson. When the theatre reopened after reconstruction in 1959, its inaugural production was Gielgud's renowned Shakespearean program *The Ages of Man*. His most recent association with the theatre was his direction of a much acclaimed production of Noel Coward's *Private Lives* with Maggie Smith and Robert Stephens, in 1974.

**10**

**Gielgud Theatre**

*Next down the line is The Gielgud theatre, which opened as the Hicks Theatre in 1906, on the corner of **Rupert Street** and Shaftesbury Avenue.* It became The Globe in 1909 and The Gielgud in 1994. In keeping with the traditional image of the street, most of the successes at the theatre have been moderately long runs of fairly lightweight comedies or romances sprinkled here and there with an occasional classic or serious play. Its first real long run appears to have been an early (1923) Somerset Maugham piece called *Our Betters*, which ran for over 500 performances. Other 500-performance shows were C.L. Anthony's *Call It a Day* in 1935, and *Robert's Wife* in 1938. Sir John brought his classic production of *The Importance of Being Earnest* to its boards in 1939, when he played John Worthing, Peggy Ashcroft played Cecily, and Dame Edith Evans put a stamp for all time on the role of Lady Bracknell.

Luckier than its counterpart The Queen's, The Globe remained active throughout the war years and offered successful productions of *Thunder Rock, Dear Brutus,* and *The Petrified Forest.* One of the major critical landmarks of the post-war era was the 1949 production of Christopher Fry's *The Lady's Not For Burning* directed by and

**10**

149

**Apollo Theatre**

starring Mr. Gielgud. This production also featured a performance by a young Welsh actor by the name of Richard Burton. The fifties saw *An Evening With Bea Lillie* and Emlyn Williams in *Dylan Thomas Growing Up*. The early sixties saw the opening of Paul Scofield in Robert Bolt's *A Man For All Seasons* and long runs of Jean Kerr's Mary Mary and Peter Shaffer's *The Private Ear and Public Eye*.

*The **Apollo Theatre**, a bit further along, opened its doors in 1901. Its frontage is in French Renaissance style and features a plethora of niches, pillars, and neo-classic figures. With a fresh coat of paint in the early nineties it now gleams in the noon sun like polished ivory.* The interior has changed little since its opening aside from periodical redecoration. Built originally as a home for musicals, the roster for the early years includes few recognizable names. In recent years the fare has been mainly comedies, romances, and an occasional thriller. Some of the post-war titles have been *Idiot's Delight, Gas Light, Cradle Song, Private Lives, Butterflies Are Free, The Owl and The Pussycat, Lulu,* and *Dial M for Murder*.

*The oldest theatre of the four is the cream and red brick Lyric, which opened in 1888.* Perhaps the first major event of historical importance in the theatre's life occurred in 1893 when the great Italian actress, Eleonora Duse made her first London appearance in *La Dame aux Camelias*. During her stay she also appeared in Goldoni's *La Locandiera (The Mistress of the Inn)* and in Ibsen's *A Doll's House*. Another international star, and Duse's great rival, Sarah Bernhardt, appeared here in 1898.

Musicals interspersed with classical seasons kept the theatre running throughout the first 30 years of the new century. In 1933, just after a major renovation, the theatre had a string of American successes including Alfred Lunt and Lynn Fontanne in Robert Sherwood's *Reunion in Vienna,* Sydney Kingsley's *Men in White,* and Kaufman and Ferber's *Theatre Royal.* The two major post-war hits were the 476 performance run of Terence Rattigan's *The Winslow Boy* in 1946-47 and the John Clements-Kay Hammond revival of *The Beaux Stratagem* in 1948-49. Then it was time for the long run champion to open. *The Little Hut* ran for 1,261 performances. More recent shows have been *Cactus Flower, Plaza Suite, Habeas Corpus, Five Guys Called Moe,* and a rock musical starring Gerry and the Pacemakers called *Ferry Across the Mersey*. In 1997 it housed the transfer of the RSC's *Cyrano de Bergerac,* starring Antony Sher.

*Just past The Lyric on your left is the entrance to one of Picadilly's newer entertainment complexes, the Trocadero. Explore it if you wish; otherwise continue down Shaftesbury Avenue to the next traffic light, where* **Great Windmill Street** *angles off into the heart of "seamy" Soho. Look to your right. An ancient and not so honorable Soho landmark,* **The Windmill Theatre,** *used to stand up there, but is now dark.*

*Next comes a possible diversion. If you wish to see a bit more of what is left of the gritty side of Soho, take a trip up Great Windmill Street. If this is not your cup of tea, simply read the next paragraph on The Windmill Theatre from here and continue on down Shaftesbury Avenue until it arrives at Piccadilly Circus. When you arrive at the circus take a sharp left and head down* **Coventry Street** *toward* **Leicester Square** *where our walk will terminate.*

*For those taking the side trip, walk up Great Windmill Street. The site of the theatre is supposed to have been on the location of a mill on a path that led up the slight hill from Piccadilly and the top of the Haymarket.* Originally built in 1910 as a cinema, it was completely re-designed as a legitimate theatre in 1931. After some hit-and-miss productions and a brief return to films, a non-stop variety and revue format was inaugurated. This developed into a burlesque-style entertainment that featured comedy acts, dancing girls, and judicious nude tableaus. The proud claim during the Blitz was that "We Never Closed" and indeed the Windmill was the only theatre in London that did not miss a performance during the entire Second World War

**10**

except for twelve compulsory closure days from September 4 to 16 of 1939. During the worst of the Blitz, the performers often slept nightly inside the theatre rather than risking travel on the streets during the bombings. The entertainment formulated at the Windmill was termed "Revudeville" and breathed its last in 1964. For a long time after that it was basically a strip club, but in its post-war years could claim to have launched the careers of then unknown comedians like Tony Hancock, Harry Secombe and Peter Sellers.

*Continue with the diversion to the top of Great Windmill Street. Turn right at **Brewer Street***. *You are now in the heart of old seamy steamy Soho and it still isn't exactly Mary Poppins land. At **Rupert Street** is a left turn into the pedestrian path called Walker's Court. A short stroll through the porn shops will take you out into the **Berwick Street Market**— a lively and cheap place to buy fruits and vegetables. If you turn right at this corner you can stroll through the Rupert Street flea market as you return to Shaftesbury Avenue. Cross it and continue on until you run into **Coventry Street** at the very edge of **Leicester Square**.*

*However you have reached Leicester Square, work your way into the grassy center near the Shakespeare statue.* The square has been cleared of the glassy-eyed winos, hustlers, and drug dealers that had created a less than savory ambience throughout the 1980s. Now it mainly

appears to be full of young tourists chowing down on Burger King Whoppers and slices of pizza. *If you can find a bench sit a spell. On a pleasant day you might even hear the birds sing.*

Up until the 1600s this area was reserved for common grazing lands. Building started when the Earl of Leicester got permission to put his house approximately where the Empire Cinema is today. By the 1700s the square was built up completely and at various times contained the homes of fashionable and successful men from all walks of life, including Dr. John Hunter, a famous

**Walker's Court**

surgeon, the scientist Sir Isaac Newton, and the artists Hogarth and Joshua Reynolds. *Today their busts occupy the corners of the garden square that was laid out in 1874 just as the area was developing into the music hall and cabaret center of the West End. The centerpiece of the square is, incongruously, that monument to William Shakespeare. His rather cloying statue peers benignly out at the chaos from under its thick coating of pigeon droppings and carries a somewhat amused grin on its face. Opposite the statue of Shakespeare, but looking away from him to the left, is a small bronze statue of Charlie Chaplin, in his costume as the little tramp, complete with cane. It is the work of John Doubleday, and was unveiled by Sir Ralph Richardson in April 1981.*

**Shakespeare statue in Leicester Square**

The juxtaposition of this island of grass and flowers with its surrounding neon jungle is well worth some meditation. Today the entertainment is primarily chain restaurants, cinemas, street buskers, and pickpockets. A century ago, as the music hall center of the West End, it probably had much the same atmosphere. In their prime, the great Empire and Alhambra music halls of the turn of the century attracted some five to seven thousand people nightly into these environs. And even then when large numbers of people congregated to eat, drink, and be merry there was also an accompanying cadre of street people ranging from musicians and panhandlers to pickpockets and worse. It was all there then and it is indisputably still here now.

*But don't let that deter you from our real reason for ending at Leicester Square. London's own half-price theatre ticket booth is now located in a nice little stone*

**Charlie Chaplin statue in Leicester Square**

**10**

153

**Half Price
Ticket Booth**

*building at the bottom of the square, and if you have timed your walk
right, you can join the queue to pick up some of the best live entertainment bargains in the western world.* The booth is run by SWET, the
Society of West End Theatres, and offers half price (plus a small service charge that was two pounds per ticket in 1996) current-day tickets to any live West End performances that are not sold out. Opening
time is 1:00 PM. Don't worry if the queue seems long; it moves quite
quickly after the windows open. You must pay cash (that's English
Pounds)—no credit cards or travelers checks—and you can buy only
current day tickets to the shows that are listed on the board.

No tickets, other than those hawked by the scalpers who hang
around the queues, will be available for the latest hot musicals. Your
best bet for seats to the really popular shows is to order them through
a legitimate ticket agency and pay the surcharge, or better yet go to
or call the theatre's box office directly. The best half-price bargains
in Leicester Square are to shows that have been running a while and
are not now selling out, or shows that are in preview or have just
opened and are not selling out. You'll also find a lot of tickets for
long running comedies and second level musicals that continue to
run on the basis of tourist group bookings. One hundred tickets for
productions at the National Theatre are kept back for sale on the day
of performance, but if you really want those, it is advisable to join
the queue at the Royal National Theatre itself not later than 9 AM.

Be warned that the half-price tickets sold in Leicester Square generally are the top price tickets that normal people who pay full price
aren't eager to buy, thus a lot of the tickets come from Row 1 or
Row 2 or the side or rear of the stalls. You will see things up close
and dirty and you may get a stiff neck.

**10**

154

For those of you on a true starvation budget, it is often easier to get a cheaper seat overall by going to the theatre and buying one at list price in the Upper Circle or Gallery.

*Your tour of the "Not So Bright Lights of Soho" is now complete. Should you not be planning to get theatre tickets now, tube or bus transportation is close at hand (**Leicester Square or Piccadilly Circus tube stations**) to take you back to your lodgings. If you have decided to join the ticket queue or have some more time to read, a more detailed theatrical history of the Leicester Square area follows.*

*On the east flank of the square is the 2300 seat **Odeon Cinema** which has been operating since 1937.* It was on this site in 1854 that the Royal Panoptikon of Science and Art was constructed. This was an entertainment and display area designed to be a model of "Moorish grandeur." The external face was rounded off with two 100-foot minarets at each corner, and the interior was finished in an ornate Saracenic style. The central core of the building was a nearly 100-foot domed rotunda with a giant fountain in the middle. Around and below were exhibits of machinery, manufactured goods, and displays devoted to the latest scientific discoveries. A gigantic organ dominated one corner of the dome.

The Exhibition Center fell on hard times by 1857 and was finally auctioned off. The huge organ was sent to St. Paul's Cathedral and the building was outfitted for circuses and equestrian spectacles. In line with its Moorish architecture it was renamed The Alhambra when it was reopened in 1858. It was refitted again in 1860 as the Alhambra Palace Music Hall. The old organ gallery was remodeled into a good-sized proscenium stage with 100 feet of fly space. The pit floor was furnished with tables, and with the gallery seating on the perimeters, the capacity was upwards of 3500 patrons. The early 1860s saw more new managements, a further refitting to increase the seating capacity to 4000 people, and another new name— The Alhambra Palace of Varieties. The programs were mainly music and dancing. Since some of the presentations did involve pantomimic action and since some did stretch the bounds of contemporary propriety, the theatre also had a series of licensing problems. In 1871 they lost their music and dance license and got a drama license. The tables were removed from the pit and replaced by seats and the bars were moved into locations that were out of view of the stage. Another remodeling in 1882 added new galleries and seating in the balconies. This was completed just in time for a disastrous fire that gutted the entire building except for the exterior walls.

The Alhambra was rebuilt within a year. It retained the old front and the Moorish towers, but the interior was formed into a standard music hall with seating for about 4000. It saw a lot of popular ballet, acrobatics, and then some outstanding serious ballet companies including Diaghilev's Ballet Russes de Monte Carlo. Finally, after almost sixty years as one of the entertainment centers of London, the

**10**

155

Empire Cinema &
Dance Hall

building was sold to the Odeon circuit of cinemas in 1936 and torn
down to make way for a palace dedicated to the 20th century equiv-
alent of music hall—the motion picture.

*On the north side of the square you now see the Empire Cinema and
Dance Hall.* This site has also been given over to entertainment since
early in the 1800s when an old palatial home, Saville House, was reconstructed into an assortment of wine bars, dancing rooms, billiard parlors, revue stages, restaurants, etc. By 1848 this complex had a name,
the Salle Valentino, and according to advertisements at the time some
2000 people could trip the light fantastic in the main dance hall and
wander about through the small parlors that featured wrestlers, ven-
triloquists, fortune tellers, magic shows, etc.

In 1865 the Salle Valentino burned to the ground. It was rebuilt
as the Royal London Panorama. At one point the operation featured
an exhibition of the Charge of the Light Brigade painted on a huge
15,000-square-foot circular canvas. A series of remodelings went on
during the 1870s and 1880s, ending in a standard proscenium theatre called the Empire in 1884. This was a 3500-seat house with a

**10**

32-foot proscenium stage. The bill of fare was varied but always musical. Contemporary ballets like *Giselle* and *Coppelia* were alternated with popular spectacles like a version of Jules Verne's *Around the World in Eighty Days* complete with live elephants and a chorus of four hundred singers.

In 1887 the programming turned more toward the music hall as the managership moved to the famous Edward and Augustus Harris. The theatre became the Empire Theatre of Varieties. Like the Alhambra, the Empire was a lively meeting place for all the high-spirited and hot-blooded gallants of the town. The galleries of both theatres had "promenades" where high class "ladies of the evening" circulated and vied for the attention of the rakes in the bars or the pit. The moral situation got so bad at the Empire in 1894 that the London County Council under pressure from an American social reformer, Mrs. Ormiston Chant, closed the theatre and demanded that the "promenades" be screened off from the auditorium.

Mander and Mitchenson report that young Winston Churchill and some of his fellow cadets from Sandhurst were attending the Empire not long after it had been reopened. They discovered that the new "promenade" barriers were nothing but flimsy fabric screens that could be easily punctured by a gentleman's walking stick. Hole poking was soon much too mild and it did not take long before the young men were tearing the screens out of their moorings. Churchill made one of his maiden speeches then and there against the council edicts and proceeded to lead the unruly mob out into the streets to parade up Piccadilly carrying the broken pieces of screening as banners.

After a major renovation in 1904, the presentations turned more to musical revues and then to musicals. The last show to run at the old Empire was George Gershwin's *Lady Be Good* with Fred and Adele Astaire. The wreckers moved in quickly and by 1928 the first Empire Cinema opened on the site. This was a 3500-seat movie palace with a fully equipped proscenium stage so that variety acts and music could also be accommodated. From 1949 to 1952 the Empire played a half film and half music-dance-revue program. It was closed in 1961 and remodeled into a large two-story dance hall with stage (now the Empire Dance Hall) and into the smaller 1300-seat cinema that still bears the Empire name.

**10**

*A final important lost London Theatre that stood just off the northeast corner of the square between Cranbourn and Lisle streets was Daly's Theatre.* It was called Daly's Theatre after the U.S. producer and impresario Augustus Daly and was built by George Edwardes, the manager of the famous Gaiety Theatre, for use by Daly's company. Daly had been bringing his American company to London each year from 1884 to 1891 and Edwardes sought to build the theatre and lease it to Daly at a profit, which he did for a few years. Daly's Theatre opened in 1893 and was the first theatre in London to be built on the cantilever principle, thus eliminating the posts that would normally have been necessary to hold up the balconies or circles. It had an Italian Renaissance frontage and a Rococo interior with seats for 1200 patrons. Daly opened the theatre with his production of *Taming of the Shrew*. Eleonora Duse and Sarah Bernhardt both performed there in 1894. During the early part of the 20th century the house was known primarily for musicals and operettas. Finally in 1937 Warner Brothers bought the site and remodeled it into a 1700-seat cinema.

Here's hoping that by now the ticket line is moving along and that your particular favorite is up on the board. Have a pleasant afternoon or evening at the theatre.

A final note. There are at least fifty or more fringe/outlying theatres in London. The quality varies but some truly exciting things are going on outside the West End. Fringe tickets are never sold at the half-price booth, but most of them will take telephone orders and even credit cards. Your cost will seldom go over ten pounds and can be as small as three or four pounds. Your source for fringe theatre programming and just about everything else in London is the weekly *Time Out* magazine. Buy one as soon as you hit town.

**10**

WALK ELEVEN

# Take a Stroll in Residential Kensington and Holland Park

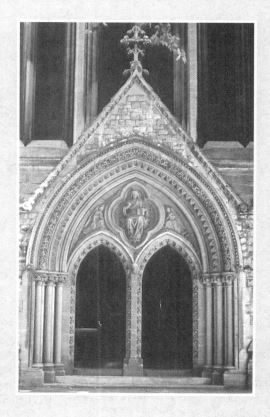

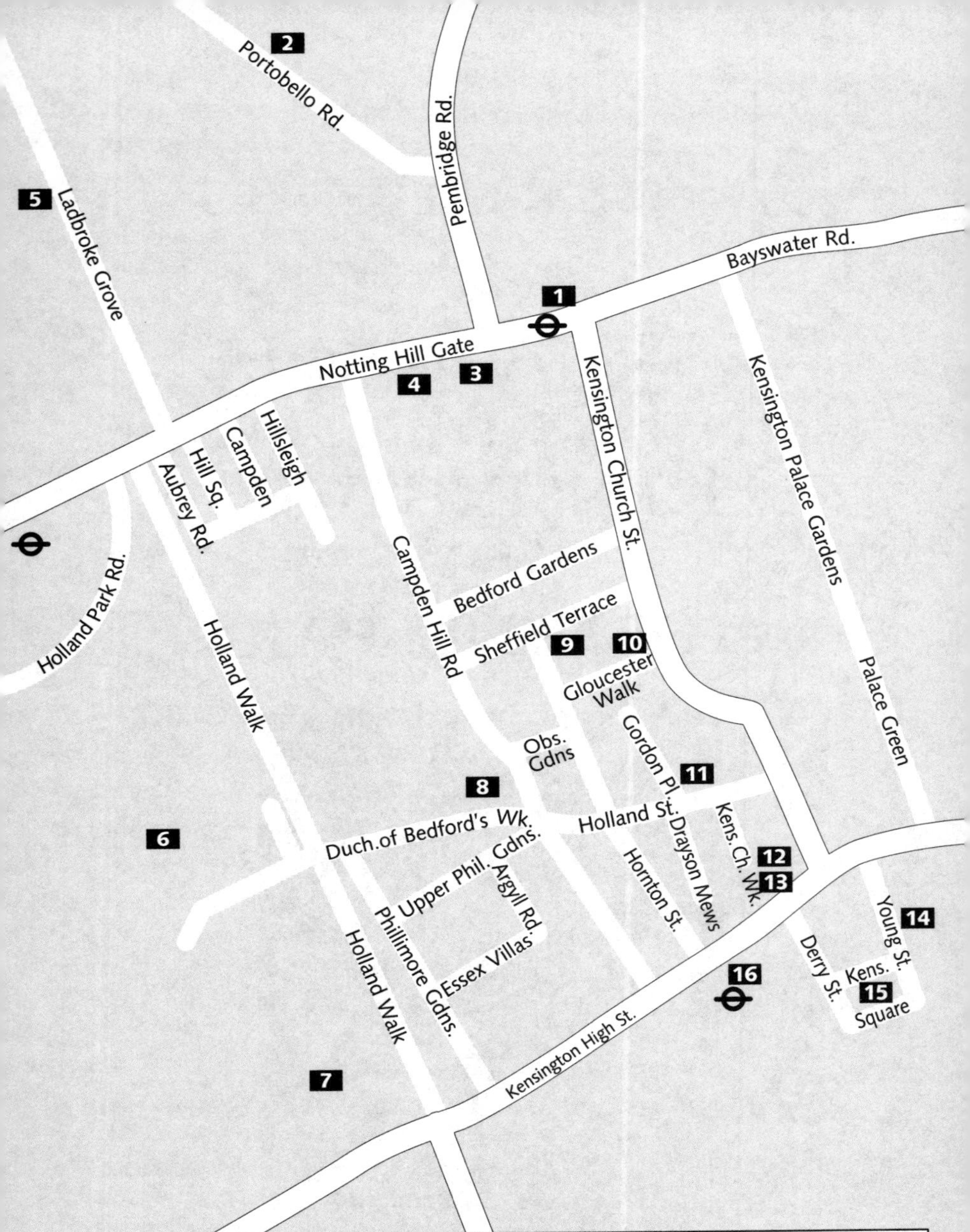

**Map labels:**

Portobello Rd.

Pembridge Rd.

Ladbroke Grove

Bayswater Rd.

Notting Hill Gate

Kensington Church St.

Kensington Palace Gardens

Palace Green

Hillsleigh Rd.

Campden Hill Sq.

Aubrey Rd.

Holland Park Rd.

Holland Walk

Campden Hill Rd.

Bedford Gardens

Sheffield Terrace

Gloucester Walk

Obs. Gdns

Gordon Pl.

Holland St.

Drayson Mews

Kens. Ch. Wk.

Duch. of Bedford's Wk.

Upper Phil. Gdns.

Argyll Rd.

Essex Villas

Phillimore Gdns.

Holland Walk

Hornton St.

Kens. Ch. Wk.

Young St.

Kens. Square

Derry St.

Kensington High St.

Warwick

## Walk Eleven

1 Notting Hill Gate Station
2 Portobello Antique Market
3 Gate Cinema
4 Coronet Cinema
5 St. John's Ladbroke Grove
6 Holland Park
7 Commonwealth Institute
8 King's College London
9 Green Lodge
10 J. M. Barrie and Jean Sibelius residence
11 The Elephant & The Castle
12 Ezra Pound residence
13 St. Mary Abbot's Church
14 Thackeray residence
15 Kensington Square
16 High Street Kensington Tube Station

⊖ Tube Station

**STARTING POINT:** Notting Hill Gate Station (District, Circle, or Central Line).

**APPROXIMATE TIME:** Two to three hours depending on how much time you spend in the park.

T oo often the visitor to London gets trapped by the major monuments, the shopping streets, and the entertainment centers. In this swirl of noise and business you can forget that real people live in London and if they live in Kensington they do it with a certain panache. This area has appealed to artists and literary people for over a hundred years. The walk doesn't have a lot of theatre references, but it takes you through an enchanting neighborhood park (Holland Park), an immaculately kept and architecturally fascinating residential neighborhood, a lovely church, and an oddity on top of a building.

If you should choose a Saturday for this walk and are interested in antiques, Notting Hill Gate is very close to the famous Portobello Road Antique market. If interested in this side trip, take a right at **Pembridge Road** after you exit the tube station. You will shortly pass the Prince Albert pub, home of the Gate Theatre. Keep going, watching for **Portobello Road** intersecting on your left. Turn into it and follow it or the crowds until the market comes into view.

T ake the tube to **Notting Hill Gate**. After clearing the exit turnstiles, take the left turn to the street and mount the right hand stairs. You should emerge on the south side of the street and begin to stroll west (straight ahead) toward **Holland Park Avenue**. You will pass the **Gate and Coronet** cinemas and then quickly the street will turn from commercial to residential. You will pass **Campden Hill Road** and **Hillsleigh Road** on your way. Watch for the gates on #17 and #19 with their pine cones and owls. Not too much further will be **Campden Hill Square**. Turn left up the hill. On your right is a lovely wooded park that makes a private garden for the terrace houses that surround the square. If the wooded area is on your left and the houses on the right, you have gone one street too far. This square was laid out in 1826 and many of the houses date from shortly after that time. The heavy iron fencing around

11

161

**Spire of St. John's Ladbroke Grove**

the central park is original and the wrought iron work and the door and window treatments on the houses are exquisitely varied.

The famous English painter J. M. W. Turner used to come to a friend's home on this hill because it was such a marvelous place from which to paint the sunset. *When you reach the top of the square, turn right. At #16 a blue plaque records that Charles Morgan, a novelist and critic, lived here from 1894-1932. At #23 a blue plaque trumpets the residence of Siegfried Sassoon from 1925-1932, which was inhabited by the Davies family around the turn of the century.* Nothing exciting about them, but their young children inspired J.M. Barrie to write his most famous work, *Peter Pan.*

*Continue on straight ahead until the street ends at **Aubrey Road**. Turn right and head back down the hill. Here you will see nicely kept houses of more modest proportion. They are one block off the square. Nicely framed between the buildings ahead of you is the spire of **St. John's Ladbroke Grove** (1845). When you arrive back at Holland Park Avenue again, turn left, cross Aubrey Road and walk no more than about twenty yards further. You are looking on your left for the entrance to narrow little **Holland Walk**. Take it and start up the hill. Make sure that you stay out of the bike path. Initially this walkway is hemmed in by brick walls but soon the right side will give way to the green of **Holland Park**. You can sense the difference almost immediately. Blackberry bushes crowd up to the fence, songbirds cry, and occasionally you'll hear from beyond the green leaves the sound of laughing children. Look for the first opening in the fence (on your right) and take it into the park, where you can continue your stroll down a pleasant tree shaded path.*

*Keep your eyes to the right and soon another path and the Tudor gables of what remains of Holland House will appear through the trees. This lovely old country home was almost totally destroyed by bombs during World War II and today houses a youth hostel. There is sadly nothing to see and you need not follow that path.*

The Holland Estate (roughly covering the area of the current park) was owned by the DeVere family, Earls of Oxford, until the time of James I. One owner, Edward DeVere (1550-1604), has had the

**11**

**Holland Park**

distinction of being advanced by a contemporary relative as a possible author for Shakespeare's plays. The house continued its theatrical connections on into the Commonwealth, when it reportedly was the site of bootleg performances after Cromwell and his men had closed the public theatres. Joseph Addison, author of the tragedy *Cato* and co-author with Richard Steele of the famous Spectator, lived in the house from 1716 to his death in 1719.

In the middle of the 18th century the house was sold to Henry Fox, father of the great politician and orator, Charles James Fox. Fox was made Baron Holland in 1763 and he made Holland House into a center of political and literary activity. Theatrical figures, including Richard Brinsley Sheridan, John Philip Kemble, and Edmund Kean, were regular visitors.

Even today the arts continue to be associated with the park. The Orangery is often the scene of jazz concerts and poetry readings and there is an open air theatre for opera and musical concerts.

**11**

*Continue walking straight ahead past the school until you reach another major crossing path. There is an exit to the left called* **The Duchess of Bedford's Walk** *that will take you out of the park.* **Remember this spot. You must return to it in order to continue the walk after you make a foray deeper into the park.** *You will find lovely gardens (both traditional English and Japanese, childrens' play areas, parading peacocks, and other surprises. Summer and winter the park is full of real Londoners of all ages and nationalities.*

Take a right turn away from the exit, which will put you along the top of the playing fields. At the bottom of the fields is the massive green copper roof of the **Commonwealth Institute,** a museum and cultural center devoted to the countries of the British Commonwealth. Visit it only if you have plenty of time. On the right you will pass the open air theatre, where you can enjoy opera in the summer months.

At the next intersection past the theatre continue to walk ahead. There'll be some tables and a snack bar to your right and off to the left an honest to goodness working drinking water fountain. Across from the fountain is a building with a large signboard on it. It contains a map of the whole park and even lists what flowers are in bloom and where. Here you can make a decision about what other parts of the park you wish to see. There's also a loo in the building. It's around to the side fronting on the children's play area. The men's room contains a scale and for ten pence you can find out how many stone you weigh. And ultimately remember you must get back to the exit at the Duchess of Bedford's Walk that leads out of the park.

You should now have taken your pastoral pleasure and returned to the exit. Upon leaving the park gate jog about ten yards to the left and then turn right almost immediately down **Phillimore Gardens.** You are thrust slam bang quickly into monumental, neo-classic, gleaming

Kensington. Walk on for three short blocks. Turn left at **Essex Villas.** At #8 on the right lived W.S. Gilbert (1836-1911), famed librettist and partner of Arthur Sullivan. Turn left at the end of Essex Villas up **Argyll Road.** Jog to the right on **Upper Phillimore Gardens** at the top of Argyll Road. You'll shortly arrive at the five point intersection of **Campden Hill Road.**

The obviously modern looking warren of buildings to your right are the Kensington Town Hall and Library.

**W. S. Gilbert residence**

11

**Restored Victorian flats**

*You should turn left, cross the Duchess of Bedford's Walk again and proceed up Campden Hill Road. As you walk, the buildings of* **Kings College-London** *(formerly Queen Elizabeth College) are on your left. At* **Observatory Gardens** *you will want to feast your eyes on a lovingly restored Victorian flat block.* Note in particular the ornate carvings, the mansard roof, and the wrought iron detailing. Corin Redgrave of the famous Redgrave acting family used to live there. Kate Terry, the eldest of another great theatrical dynasty, lived at Moray Lodge on Campden Hill after her marriage to Arthur Lewis and retirement from the stage. Her sister Ellen was the most famous member of her siblings, but Marion, Florence and Fred also made their mark, as of course did Kate's grandson, John Gielgud.

*At or just behind #78 Campden Hill Road, novelist and playwright John Galsworthy (1867-1933) lived for a while in 1903. At the next house #80 you can also see a blue plaque identifying the former residence of novelist and critic Ford Madox Ford (1873-1939). Continuing up Campden Hill Road you will soon come to Sheffield Terrace. Turn right and go down to number 58.* Note the carved unicorn and lion over the front door. In it lived for many years one of the world's most famous mystery writers, Agatha Christie. She also authored the world's longest running play, The Mousetrap. It opened in 1952 and looks as if it will run well into the next century.

*Turn around and return to* **Campden Hill Road.** *Take a right, walk another block to* **Bedford Gardens,** *then turn right again.* This street is a treasure of fascinating houses. #87-91 have wrought iron balconies

**11**

Left: John Galsworthy residence
Right: Agatha Christie residence
Lower right: Ezra Pound residence

that seem right out of New Orleans. #54 has a covered walkway from the street to the front door. #5 was once the home of Richard Le Gallienne, a literary historian and poet. Theatre buffs may be more familiar with his daughter Eva Le Gallienne. She came to New York in 1915 and made a considerable reputation for herself as an actress and producer-director. She was instrumental in popularizing Ibsen in the United States during the 1930s and in the 1940s was a co-founder of the American Repertory Theatre. Number 4 bears a blue plaque to the composer Frank Bridge, who lived here.

*Follow Bedford Gardens through to **Kensington Church Street,** turn right and go down the hill for two blocks to **Gloucester Walk**. Turn right. **J.M. Barrie,** author of* Peter Pan *and* The Admirable Crichton *lived on this block in 1892 and so did the composer **Jean Sibelius**.*

*Turn left when you reach the tee intersection of **Hornton Street,** and follow it downhill until you reach the back of the Public Library. At **Holland Street** turn left. Don't be confused by the street number on the southeast corner house. Number 43 has been crossed out and 54 painted in above it. Walk up Holland Street and feast your eyes on residential London in all of its variety. On your right peek into **Drayson Mews**. Next is a charming, gardened cul de sac called **Gordon Place**. Kitty corner* *from this jewel of a street is a pleasant neighborhood pub, **The Elephant and The Castle**, where you can sit outside on a bench under a cascade of flowers and enjoy a pint on a sunny afternoon or evening. The next tiny street is **Kensington Church Walk**. Take a right turn into it. It is quiet, elegant, and lined with speciality shops. At number 10 the poet Ezra Pound lived.*

*The lane opens out into a lovely hidden garden tucked in behind Sir Gilbert Scott's **St. Mary Abbot's Church**. At 278* feet its spire is the tallest in London. Buried somewhere in its churchyard are the Restoration theatre manager and actor, Thomas Killigrew (1612-1693); George Colman the Elder (1732-1836), a play-wright and theatre manager; and Mrs. Elizabeth Inchbald

**St. Mary Abbot's Church**

(1753-1821), actress and dramatist. Should the church be open it is well worth a look, though its dark and gloomy Victorian atmosphere is a lowering contrast to the uplifting lightness of Wren's interiors that are visited in Walk Nine.

*If you move through the covered cloister that leads out from the east side of the church (push on the cloister door if it is not open), you will find yourself out into the traffic and the noise of **Kensington High Street**. Should the cloister be locked **Kensington Church Walk** will jog to the right and also gain you access to the High Street.*

*Cross the always busy Kensington High Street toward Barker's department store. Turning left on the south side of the street proceed to the next corner, which is **Young Street**, and turn right. Cross over to the left side of the street so you can see clearly the pleasant house, number 16, where **William Thackeray** (1811-1863) lived and wrote* Vanity Fair, *commemorated by a brown plaque. Shortly you will reach once fashionable **Kensington Square**, which was laid out in 1685 for the Courtiers who wished to live near the Royal Family at Kensington Palace. The French politician Talleyrand lived in the square for a while in the 1790s. John Stuart Mill, the philosopher, had a residence at number 18. Turn right and traverse one side of the square. Kitty corner to your left is number 33, the home for many years of Mrs. Patrick Campbell, actress and friend*

**11**

Top left: William Thackeray residence
Top right Mrs. Patrick Campbell
        residence
Left: Roof garden of Derry & Tom's

of *G.B. Shaw, marked by a drab square brown plaque.* The part of Liza Doolittle in *Pygmalion* was created for her by Shaw and their long correspondence was published after Shaw's death. The letters were made into a dramatic work called *Dear Liar* by Jerome Kilty in 1960.

*Turn right and you are now headed back toward Kensington High Street on **Derry Street**. At number 99 on the left is the entrance to one of London's little known oddities, the old roof gardens of the long defunct Derry and Toms department store, which are sometimes still accessible during the day. Ask the security man if you can take a peek. Once on top of the building you can stroll through a set of landscaped gardens complete with trees, ponds, live ducks, and fountains.*

*If gardens in the air are not your cup of tea, you can walk immediately back to the High Street and turn left. **The High Street Kensington Tube Station** (District and Circle Lines) is to your left and your stroll through residential Kensington is finished.*

**11**

# WALK TWELVE

# COVENT GARDEN PROMENADE

## Map Labels

Charing Cross Rd.
Kingsway
Monmouth St.
Neal St.
Shorts Gdns.
20
Drury Ln.
Kemble St.
Shaftesbury Ave.
Earlham
16
15
17
19
Kean St.
Bow St.
St.
James St.
21
22
Aldwych
14
13
West St.
Upper St. Martin's Ln.
18
Long Acre
Floral St.
25
26
Russell Ln.
Catherine St.
24
Grt. Newpt.
4
King St.
28
29
Wellington St.
23
6
Garrick St.
5
27
Henrietta Gdns.
Tavistock St.
St.
7
1
New Row St.
9
St. Martin's Ct. 8
Cranbourn
10
Bedford St.
Maiden Ln.
11
Lower Charing Cross Rd.
Lower St. Martin's Ln.
2
Strand
12
3
Pall Mall E.
Trafalgar Square

RIVER THAMES

## Walk Twelve

1 Leicester Square Tube Station
2 Coliseum Theatre
3 St. Martin-in-the-Fields
4 Stanford's
5 Garrick Club
6 Lamb & Flag
7 Albery Theatre
8 Salisbury Pub
9 Wyndham's Theatre
10 Duke of York's Theatre
11 Garrick Theatre
12 National Portrait Gallery
13 St. Martin's Theatre
14 Ambassadors Theatre
15 Seven Dials
16 Cambridge Theatre
17 Donmar Warehouse Theatre
18 Covent Garden Tube Station
19 Kemble's Head Pub
20 Prince of Wales Pub
21 Fortune Theatre
22 Aldwych Theatre
23 Duchess Theatre
24 Drury Lane Theatre
25 Globe Pub
26 Covent Garden/Royal Opera House
27 St. Paul's Covent Garden
28 London Transport Museum
29 Theatre Museum
⊖ Tube Station

T*his long three part walk takes you to a number of important West End theatre venues (the Coliseum, Drury Lane, and Royal Opera House), passes by several book, print, and memorabilia shops, schedules stops at the National Portrait Gallery, Covent Garden Market, and the Actors' Church (St. Paul's Covent Garden), visits some atmospheric pubs, and finishes at the Theatre Museum. Begin this journey no earlier than 9:30 AM so the shops will be open, and plan to spend the day. Avoid Mondays for Part III, as the Theatre Museum is closed.*

## PART I

L*eave the* **Leicester Square tube station** *via the* **Charing Cross Road** *South exit. Turn right a few paces, then right again to access* **Cranbourn Street***. Walk to the next inter-section. Look to your left to see* **Great Newport Street** *and a blue plaque honoring the painter Sir Joshua Reynolds. Cross the street toward it.*

*From this vantage point you should be able to see the mar-quee for the Unicorn Theatre for Children.* This used to be The Arts Theatre and was home of The Arts Theatre Club. It was built in 1927 and was designed as a Club Theatre. Its stated purpose was to provide meal amenities, a congenial gathering place for

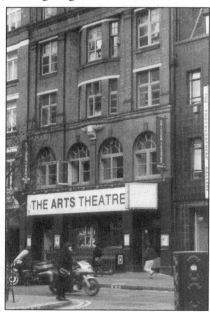

Arts Theatre (now the Unicorn Theatre for Children)

**12**

171

people interested in theatre, and a small auditorium (339 seats) to stage new, challenging, or provocative plays that might not have sufficient drawing power to justify a larger West End theatre. In 1968 the "club" distinction became unnecessary when the government finally abolished the requirement to submit play scripts to the Lord Chamberlain for approval.

In its "club" guise the Arts did play a significant role in modern English dramatic history. In 1955 the directorship of the Arts Theatre opened up. John Fernald had resigned to become head of RADA (Royal Academy of Dramatic Art) and George Devine rejected an offer to replace him because he preferred taking over the English Stage Company at the Royal Court Theatre. By default the job was offered to a young (age 24) university graduate who was working at the Club as a play reader. His name was Peter Hall and his staging later that year of the English premiere of Samuel Beckett's *Waiting for Godot* made his reputation and propelled him onto the fast track that was to lead to the directorship of the Royal Shakespeare Theatre and then the Royal National Theatre.

In 1966 Caryl Jenner and her Unicorn Theatre for Children took over the premises. It runs under this name today with occasional productions by other managements.

*Turn away from the Arts Theatre now and address yourself to the chaos of the six-sided intersection surrounding you. To your left is **Upper St. Martin's Lane**. We will return to this spot and explore that area in Part Two of this walk. **Lower St. Martin's Lane** is to your right and John Gielgud maintained a flat at #7 in the 1930s. It was known to his friends as Seven Upper. A little further along the design team known as Motley had a studio.* Their third floor workspace was formerly the furniture workshop of Thomas Chippendale and already had known a number of well-off actors as customers in the 18th century. David Garrick was apparently one of those who shopped there. In the 1930s and early 1940s this was a popular gathering place for other West End actors as well as Gielgud. *In the distance on St. Martin's Lane is the shining globe of the **Coliseum Theatre** and the spire of **St. Martin-in-The-Fields**. We'll be walking by them shortly.*

*__Long Acre__ is the street straight ahead of you. Cross St. Martin's Lane to reach Long Acre and look on your right for Dillon's Arts Bookshop. A browse is certainly in order. If one bookstore is enough, simply walk through the shop and exit by the rear door on **Garrick Street**. If additional bookstores excite you, exit the Arts Bookshop through the front door and turn right. You'll find **Stanford's**, a map and travel book store, almost immediately. If both stores are closed a few more steps on Long Acre will take you to **Rose Street**. Turn right and take it through to **Floral Street**, turn right again until Floral meets Garrick Street. Go right a bit again and you'll find the rear entrance to The Arts Bookshop.*

**Garrick Club**

*From that vantage point look across the street and you'll see a rather dirty grey Italian Palazzo style building. You are staring at the* **Garrick Club** *(1860).* The club itself was founded in 1831 and was originally limited to actors, dramatists, and other theatre people. That membership has broadened considerably in the 20th century to include publishers and other professionals, but it still boasts a great many theatre people. The building was designed by F. Marrable and holds a first-rate theatre library and an extraordinary collection of theatrical paintings and sculpture. Unfortunately, as it is a private club, you may not enter unless you are the guest of a member. If you have such a connection, use it.

*Turn left now and move back toward and past Floral Street and continue up Garrick Street. Keep a sharp eye out for a left hand opening. It's called* **Rose Alley** *and nestled at the end is the delightful Georgian facade of the* **Lamb and Flag** *pub.* It was once associated with prize fighting and was called the Bucket Of Blood. Today it is a popular hangout for theatre folks and tourists. John Dryden was mugged in the alley next to the pub one night; the publican came to his rescue and dragged him inside to give him a reviving draught of fine English ale. *You'll want to make a brief visit if it is open to explore its cramped nooks and crannies.*

*Return to Garrick Street and turn left. At the next corner cross to the Garrick Club side of the street and continue into* **New Row** *toward the sign of the White Swan pub. New Row is a smashing little street full of restaurants and shops of all kinds. Follow it and stop at your pleasure. Ultimately it will carry you right back to St. Martin's Lane. You will emerge to see the* **Albery Theatre** *in front of you and a bit to the right.*

The Albery, built in 1903 by Charles Wyndham, was constructed on a vacant lot behind the 1899 Wyndham's theatre. Wyndham had already

**The Albery**

named the 1899 theatre after himself and didn't quite know what to call this one, so it became the "New Theatre" behind the old one. Or perhaps the name came from being directly across from New Row. In either case it took some seventy years before the now comfortably middle-aged New Theatre was finally given the name of Albery after Sir Bronson Albery, who was the son of Charles Wyndham. His second wife Mary Moore was the widow of the 19th century playwright James Albery. Both the Wyndham and Albery families played major roles in the management of West End theatres for most of the last 100 years.

Any pick of great plays or great seasons offered at this theatre would have to be personal, but most accounts do mention the great 1934 *Hamlet* of John Gielgud, the 1935 *Romeo and Juliet* in which Gielgud and Olivier alternated Romeo and Mercutio, and the 1944-48 Old Vic Company seasons that featured Olivier, Sybil Thorndike, and Ralph Richardson in a long series of classic performances. In the eighties the Albery was host to two well-known controversial American imports, *Torch Song Trilogy* and *The Normal Heart*.

*Just to the left of the theatre is the **Salisbury pub**, a lovingly restored Victorian castle of mirrors, cut glass, and plush red upholstery.* The Salisbury has often been called the Actors' Pub and is a popular meeting place for performers and spectators. *Cross the street and visit now if you wish or make a note to come back for lunch today as we will be returning past here to pick up Part II of the walk. Otherwise this is a must stop on some evening when you are seeing a play in the area.*

*If you are not stopping at the Salisbury now, cross the street and plunge straight ahead down **St. Martin's Court**, which runs between the Albery*

**12**

**The Salisbury Pub**

*Theatre and the pub. On the left you will shortly pass Sheekey's Restaurant, a popular pre- or post-theatre eating spot.*

*You will emerge out onto Charing Cross Road. To your immediate right is the marquee of* **Wyndham's Theatre** *and just beyond that the Leicester Square tube station where we began our walk.* Pause and consider Wyndham's Theatre for a moment. It was constructed, as we

**Wyndham's Theatre**

**Cecil Court scene**

have mentioned previously, in 1899 by the 19th century actor-manager Charles Wyndham and his leading lady (later to become his second wife) Mary Moore. The original theatre site stretched all the way back to St. Martin's Lane and this theatre was built about four years before the Albery (New Theatre). Both buildings were designed by the same well known theatre architect, W. G. R. Sprague.

From an historical perspective some of the important productions that have graced its stage have been the Joan Littlewood Stratford East transfers of Shelagh Delaney's *A Taste of Honey,* Brendan Behan's *The Hostage,* and the satiric musical *Oh What a Lovely War.* In later years it has seen Vanessa Redgrave in *The Prime of Miss Jean Brodie* and Diana Rigg in *Abelard and Heloise.*

Musicals have not been ignored and *The Boy Friend* and *Godspell* both had runs here as well. In 1975 the National Theatre transfer of Harold Pinter's *No Man's Land* with John Gielgud and Ralph Richardson had a long run prior to its American tour.

*If you are standing in front of the theatre and looking into the lobby, turn to your right (away from the tube station) and walk one short block down Lower Charing Cross Road to* **Cecil Court.** *Turn left. This pedestrian walkway is filled with book and print stores. Take your time and browse where you will. At a minimum explore David Drummond's "Theatre Ephemera and Books." Cecil Court ends at* **St. Martin's Lane** *and a right turn will bring you into a position to examine the imposing bulk of the* **Coliseum Theatre.**

The Coliseum was designed by Frank Matcham to the specifications of producer Sir Oswald Stoll, who had dreams of building a huge variety theatre in the Charing Cross area that was larger than Drury Lane in Covent Garden. It was opened in 1904 and remains to this day the largest theatre in the city, with a stated capacity of 2558 seats. The exterior style is Italian Renaissance. In addition to other amenities it originally possessed a large roof garden that was pulled down in 1951. The square tower is articulated with the roof by four pilasters and carved figures representing Art, Music, Science, and Architecture. Additional decoration proceeds skywards until at the pinnacle eight Cupids support a large illuminated globe that at one time used to revolve.

**12**

To read the accounts of this theatre in Mander and Mitchenson's *The Theatres of London* is to be continually amazed. There were lifts for the first time in Europe to take the audience to the upper parts of the building. There was a private elevator used solely to lift the King to the salon outside the Royal Box. (Of course the lift car got stuck.) There were restaurants and tea rooms, facilities for sending and receiving messages and telegrams, and even a small post office and pillar box in the Main Entrance Hall. Its huge stage had the first revolve in England—a massive table made up of three concentric rings capable of moving independently in both directions.

The Coliseum

For all of its luxury, the theatre failed as a variety house and was re-christened as a general house in 1906. By 1931 it was used mainly for revues, spectacles, and musicals. The late forties saw it host a long string of big American musicals like *Kiss Me Kate, Annie Get Your Gun, Guys and Dolls, Can Can,* and *Pajama Game.* Hard times arrived by the sixties and the theatre was converted into a showplace for the early wide-screen cinema curiosity called Cinerama. After being designated as the new West End home of the Sadler's Wells Opera company in 1968, the theatre was closed for a complete re-decoration. Later in that year it reopened. In 1974 the Sadler's Wells company became the English National Opera and the theatre operates as their home to this day. The company's stated policy is to perform both new and classic operas in English.

*If you now continue to walk down the street toward the Coliseum, you'll find on your right the **Duke of York's** theatre.* This theatre began its life in 1892 as the Trafalgar Square. Three years later it took its present name. Like a number of other theatres in the area, the Duke of York's has a resident ghost. She is named Violet Melotte, dresses all in black, and is said to be the wife of an early manager. Important

**12**

or historic runs include *The Admirable Crichton* in 1902, *Peter Pan* in 1905, and *Misalliance, The Madras House,* and *Justice* in 1910 by Messrs. Barrie, Shaw, Granville Barker, and Galsworthy respectively.

A renovation in 1979 restored the auditorium's pink, cream, and gold decor and cleared the stalls of supporting pillars. After reopening with Glenda Jackson's tour de force titled *Rose,* there was a strong production of O'Neill's *Strange Interlude* and a long run of the dance comedy *Stepping Out.* An Amer-

Duke of York's Theatre

ican highlight of the 1980s was Al Pacino starring in David Mamet's *American Buffalo.* In the mid-nineties it became the temporary home of the Royal Court Theatre while its Sloane Square premises were being completely rebuilt. (The Royal Court Theatre Upstairs similarly found an interim base at the Ambassadors Theatre at the other end of Upper St. Martin's Lane.)

*Continue your stroll down Lower St. Martin's Lane. Take the curve to your right and swing by the back of the Edith Cavell statue in the middle of the road and start back up Lower Charing Cross Road until you reach the marquee of the* **Garrick Theatre** *named of course after the great 18th century actor David Garrick.*

With its gold leaf nicely restored in 1986, the 700-seat Garrick probably looks as good as it did when it was built in 1889. Not that it didn't have some early problems. According to Mander and Mitchenson the early excavations hit an old river known to the Romans but misplaced by the Victorians. W. S. Gilbert of Gilbert and Sullivan fame was a major investor and was said to have remarked that he wasn't sure whether to continue with the building or rent out the fishing rights.

Over the years the theatre has thrived on a mixed diet of light comedy, farce, and an occasional drama. Its longest run was achieved when the eleven year hit *No Sex Please, We're British* transferred in from

**12**

**The Garrick Theatre**

the Strand Theatre and went on to run four more years. The house ghost is said to be that of Arthur Bourchier, one of the early managers. Bourchier had an apartment at the top of the theatre and a special set of stairs that led directly to the stage. To this day he descends periodically and gently claps actors encouragingly on the back as they wait for their cues. The National Theatre smash-hit production of *An Inspector Calls* by J.B. Priestley moved here in the mid-nineties after a successful first transfer to the Aldwych, and settled into its third home for a long run.

*Turn away from the front of the Garrick now and look past a small gazebo until you locate a large* **statue of Sir Henry Irving** *(1838-1905)*. Irving was the greatest 19th century English actor/manager and, as was noted in Walk Five, the first English actor to be knighted in 1895. He was associated for years with the actress Ellen Terry at the Lyceum theatre, and their Shakespeare productions are now legendary. This statue is one of the few open-air statues of theatre people in London. Two are of Shakespeare —one in Leicester Square (Walk 10), and the other in the pocket park on the site of old St. Mary Aldermanbury (Walk 9); a third

**Statue of Henry Irving**

**12**

is the bust of Augustus Harris outside the Drury Lane theatre (coming up later in this walk) and a fourth is the bust of Sir Arthur Sullivan in the Embankment Gardens (Walk 4).

*The building directly behind Irving's statue is the **National Portrait Gallery.** Head for it and go in. The gallery contains portraits of famous British citizens from Tudor times to the present. Admission is free, the loos (go downstairs as soon as you clear security) are large and clean, and the atmosphere is generally pleasant and uncrowded. The organization is chronological: take the lift to the top floor and then simply walk down through the years. Costumiers and designers will have a field day here and the general theatre enthusiast should also find plenty to look at. Another reason to stop here would be to browse in the Gallery's excellent bookstore. They have a particularly fine collection of costume materials and quality postcards, including the exquisite portrait of the young Ellen Terry by her first husband G. F. Watts.*

*This ends Part I of the Covent Garden walk. You could easily have used up a lot of time and no one will mind if you truncate your trip right now. It's a short walk back to your left up **Lower Charing Cross Road** to the **Leicester Square tube station.***

**National Portrait Gallery**

12

From the National Portrait Gallery:

Left: William Shakespeare by John Taylor

Below: Sarah Siddons by Sir William Beechey

Bottom: The New Portrait of Alan Bennett by Tom Wood

12

Photos on this page reprinted with permission of the National Portrait Gallery.

# PART II

*F*or those pressing on, exit the National Portrait Gallery, take a few steps to your right, and use the zebra crossing to reach the island on which the statue of Edith Cavell sits. From there cross back into Lower St. Martin's Lane and head back past the Coliseum. Grab some lunch or refreshment at one of the restaurants along the way, or better yet, stop at the **Salisbury**.

Keep walking back up St. Martin's Lane until you pass that six-street intersection by the Unicorn Theatre for Children. Keep going as the street now officially becomes **Upper St. Martin's Lane**. Look for **West Street**. Guild House, home to the offices of the British Actors Equity is on the corner. Turn left.

You will shortly reach the **St. Martins** and the **Ambassadors** theatres, which between them have been home to the longest running play in London, or anywhere else for that matter. Agatha Christie's The Mousetrap opened its run on November 25, 1952, at the Ambassadors and then moved to the St. Martins in 1974, where it is still running. Although owned separately, both theatres were designed by W. G. R. Sprague, the same architect who did the Wyndham's and Albery Theatres. The Ambassadors (453 seats) was constructed first, in 1913, and the St. Martins (550 seats) followed in 1916. Now is the time to get a ticket for The Mousetrap if you haven't had the pleasure. Across the way from the Ambassadors stands the Ivy restaurant, long the favoured haunt of leading actors, from the youthful stardom of Noel Coward and John Gielgud right up to now. If your name has not been up in lights somewhere in theatreland it can be hard to secure a reservation, even for the wealthiest diners.

Turn right into Tower Court, which runs between the two theatres. Tower Court will curve a bit to the right and ultimately spill you out onto **Monmouth Street**. Look to your right for the bright gold decorated front of the Dress Circle at #57-59 Monmouth Street. It claims to be the one and only "Show Biz Stop." You'll find books, posters, CD's, scores, and lots of other good stuff.

When you exit the shop, turn right and continue up Monmouth Street until you reach the new column at infamous **Seven Dials**. This so-called circus was laid out in 1693 and was marked by an earlier column that had a sundial facing out onto each of the seven intersecting streets.

**12**

**The Ivy restaurant and the Ambassadors and St. Martins theatres**

By the 18th century the area had become one of London's worst slums. Hogarth portrayed its horrors in his engraving "Gin Lane" and Dickens described the environs in *Bleak House*. It's considerably more respectable now.

*From the center of the circus you can examine the sleek, 1930 modern* **Cambridge Theatre** *(1275 seats)*. It has not worn well. Several remodelings have not managed to give the interior much warmth and geographically the venue has always seemed detached from the West End and therefore somewhat unfashionable. Its finest hours may have been during the 1970 National Theatre season when Maggie Smith starred in Ingmar Bergman's production of *Hedda Gabler* and Laurence Olivier played Shylock to the hilt in Jonathan Miller's Victorian production of *The Merchant of Venice*.

*Move now down* **Earlham Street** *with the Cambridge Theatre at your right. On the left you will shortly see the* **Donmar Warehouse theatre.** From 1961 to 1976 the space was used as a rehearsal hall. Then from 1977 to 1981 it became a studio theatre for the Royal Shakespeare Company. While their main season played at the Aldwych theatre, the Warehouse was intended to parallel their Stratford Upon Avon experimental house, The Other Place. The most famous transfer was the 1977 *Macbeth* with Ian McKellen and Judi Dench in Trevor Nunn's legendary production—the video can be purchased in the National Theatre and other good theatre bookshops. When the RSC moved to the Barbican, the Pit fulfilled that function. Ian Albery (another member of the Albery family) took over the Donmar and formed a nonprofit company to manage it. The name derives from Ian's father

183

**The Cambridge Theatre**

Donald [Don] Albery and his friend the dancer Margot Fonteyn [Mar] and the fact that the building used to be a banana warehouse in the 19th century. Thus the Donmar Warehouse. With its 250 seats it continues to host an ever changing pastiche of new plays, experimental revivals, productions of major touring Fringe theatre companies, and general late evening musical cabarets. Ronald Bergan's *Great London Theatres* notes that the Donmar offers "genuine alternative theatre without solemnity" that seems to blend well with the mixed (age, class, and race) audiences that seem to frequent the newly revived Covent Garden entertainment area.

*Quick break time. Find an arch to your right and almost across from the Donmar Warehouse. Step up to the large plate glass window and look down. Shades of Arnold Wesker, you are looking right down on top of a restaurant kitchen.*

*A few steps further, on the Donmar Warehouse side of the street, is another diversion. There's an opening into Thomas Neal's shopping arcade. You can go through the new part and find yourself in old Neal's Yard where there are delightful outdoor cafés and healthy whole food shops. By the way all those Neal's around here commemorate Thomas Neale who laid out the Seven Dials Circus in 1693.*

*If you've explored this area, return to **Earlham Street** and turn left to proceed toward **Neal Street**. If you declined the diversion, just keep walking ahead on Earlham until you reach Neal Street and the Crown and Anchor pub. Turn right here and walk up Neal Street until you reach **Long Acre**. There are more fascinating shops along the way, such as Neal Street East which has at least seven levels stuffed with exotic merchandise from all over the world and prices range from a few pence to hundreds of pounds.*

*At Long Acre you should see the sign for the **Covent Garden Tube Station** just across the street. You will be returning there up **James Street***

**12**

*after your visit to the Theatre Museum. Once again you could easily stop here and take the tube back to your hotel, leaving the rest of the walk to be picked up at another time.*

**Right: Donmar Warehouse theatre**

**Below: Seven Dials Circus**

**12**

# PART III

To pick up here turn left for a few steps upon exiting the **Covent Garden station**. *You will shortly reach* **Long Acre**, *where you turn right. For those pressing on immediately, cross to the tube station side of the street when you reach Long Acre and turn left. At the intersection of Long Acre and* **Bow Street** *is the* **Kemble's Head pub**. There's a sign outside that gives you a nice introduction to Covent Garden history. The interior of the pub is comfortably relaxing with lush green carpet and seat cushions, a dark bar, and chocolate brown walls. Two gas logs glow invitingly and the walls are decorated with theatrical prints.

Kemble's Head pub

The official namesake here is John Philip Kemble (1757-1823). The Kemble family and their residences have been mentioned before in these pages. It was an extraordinary mini-dynasty. John Philip had a sister, Sarah (1755-1831), who performed under her married name of Siddons. She is generally considered to have been the superior performer. Charles Kemble (1775-1854) was also an actor and he had a daughter, Fanny Kemble, who made a considerable name for herself both in Britain and the United States.

John Philip Kemble is perhaps best known as the man who consolidated the managerships of both Drury Lane and Covent Garden in the early 1800s. When the Covent Garden theatre burned down in 1808, Kemble as manager put a fair amount of his own money into the reconstruction. When it reopened in 1809 he attempted to raise admission prices in the pit. Performances were interrupted for more than three months with shouts, catcalls, horns, bells, whistles,

**12**

fistfights, and even the release of a live pig in the house. Kemble ultimately capitulated and reinstated the old pit entry fees. This fracas has gone down in theatre history as the famous "OP" or "Old Price Riots."

*After looking in at the pub continue your walk for one more block up Long Acre to* **Drury Lane.** *There's a pub called* **The Prince of Wales** *on the corner across the way. Before turning right on Drury Lane you might want to cross the street and read the signboard on the pub which tells you how Drury Lane got its name.* It was originally the center of coach building activities in London, but in the 17th century it became more and more a theatrical and literary district. Samuel Pepys has a mention in his diary of walking down this street one morning and seeing Nelly Gwynn coming out of her lodgings. The critic and playwright John Dryden lived on the north side of the street from 1682 to 1686. Farther on down was the Old Queen's theatre where Henry Irving and Ellen Terry acted together for the very first time, in a shortened version of *The Taming of the Shrew.*

*As you stroll look on your right for a small pocket park called Drury Lane Gardens. It's on the former site of a burial ground dating back to 1877, but today has an enchanting playground, an actual working water fountain, and an outdoor basketball court. There is a fine explanatory sign just inside the park entrance.*

*Exit the park and turn right to continue down Drury Lane. At the corner of* **Russell Street** *you can see the 1826 colonnade along the side of the Drury Lane Theatre. We'll be coming around in front of this the-*

*atre momentarily, but for now look on your right to get a fix on the marquee of the tiny 440-seat* **Fortune Theatre.** Named after its popular Elizabethan predecessor, which was located nowhere near here(see Walk 9), this Fortune has the distinction of being an amalgamation of the church and the stage. The building is shared by the Scottish National Church and religious areas are both over and under the present theatre. It has mainly

**12**

**Fortune Theatre**

been the home of small cast show shows and its long run champion is the 1961 revue *Beyond the Fringe*. This show, besides starting a whole "satire" industry in London in the swinging sixties, launched the entertainment careers of four talented young Oxford and Cambridge graduates—Peter Cook, Dudley Moore, Jonathan Miller, and Alan Bennett.

*Cross **Russell Street** and keep going. Number 68 on your right is Brodie and Middleton—theatrical suppliers. Then at **Tavistock Street** turn right past the stage door of the **Aldwych Theatre**. Had you not have turned you would run into **Kean Street**, named after the actor Charles Kean. You also passed up a **Kemble Street** a while ago. You will shortly walk by a building, Number 89 Siddons Court, named after the actress Sarah Siddons, who was the leading tragic actress of the British stage from 1782-1812. If this isn't a theatre area nothing is.*

*When you reach **Catherine Street** you'll see the marquee of **The Duchess Theatre** across to your left.* We covered this theatre in Walk Four, but to recap, The Duchess Theatre (747 seats) dates from 1929. Two of Emlyn Williams' best plays opened here and ran for over a year each. They were *Night Must Fall* (1935) and *The Corn is Green* (1938). T. S. Eliot's *Murder in the Cathedral* had its first West End production here in 1936 and Noel Coward's *Blithe Spirit* had already run a year at the Piccadilly Theatre before it transferred to the Duchess in 1942 where it continued through 1945, running up a total of 1,997 performances.

In 1974 the nude review *Oh Calcutta!* transferred into the theatre and for the next four years the house was filled with high-class bodies and low-class jokes. The Duchess also holds the West End record for shortest run ever. The *Intimate Review,* which premiered in 1930, did not even survive its opening night. The curtain was dropped and the audience dismissed before the conclusion of the show.

*Turn right into **Catherine Street** and head for the front of the **Drury Lane Theatre** where the grand tale of Miss Saigon has been going on for more than seven years.*

*Thirsty? On the way toward the theatre you'll see the Nell of Old Drury pub across the street to your left. There are some nice theatrical prints inside. One of the tables outside on the sidewalk may be as good a place as any to read a bit about the Drury Lane Theatre. If it looks full try the Opera Tavern three doors down, another favorite with actors.* To recount even the barest story of this venerable site would take, indeed has taken, volumes. For a far more thorough presentation than we can give you here, inquire at the box office about an interior tour.

The first theatre on this site (Theatre Royal—Bridges Street) was built by Thomas Killigrew in 1663. He, you may remember if you have taken Walk Three, received one of the two Royal Patent dispensations to perform in London when Charles II returned to the English Throne in 1660. It was a long narrow building (58 by 112 feet) with a capacity of around 700. The auditorium had an open pit,

**12**

boxes, and galleries. Nell Gwynn was a performer here and Samuel Pepys attended. As W. Mac-Queen Pope says in *Ghosts and Greasepaint,* the English seem to find eating and playgoing inseparable activities. As soon as the Drury Lane started operating, it employed a professional caterer and sometime procurer, Mistress Mary Meggs, who was familiarly known as Orange Moll. She controlled the girls who sold apples and oranges to everyone except those in the top gallery. Either the unruly group in the "Gods" didn't spend

**Drury Lane Theatre**

enough to make the climb worthwhile or it just didn't pay to provide them with additional missiles. Drury Lane number one escaped the Great Fire of London in 1666 but burned down anyway in 1672.

This was actually a good break for Killigrew. In 1671 his main competitor, William Davenant, had opened the larger, better equipped, and more elegant Christopher Wren-designed Dorset Garden Theatre. After the fire, Killigrew went straight to Wren for his replacement. The Wren-designed second Drury Lane opened in 1674. This building held around 2000 people and you see prints of it often in theatre history textbooks. The auditorium had rings of boxes and rear galleries. The stage had a 17-foot apron and was 15 feet deep behind the proscenium. Christopher Rich remodeled the interior around 1695 to increase the seating. He shortened the forestage and added more boxes at the sides.

**12**

Thomas Betterton was the leading actor at the second Drury Lane in its early

**Nell of Old Drury pub**

189

years. In 1716 the building saw an assassination attempt on King George II. In 1745 Dr. Thomas Arne, music director of the theatre, composed a song in honor of George III. It was called "God Bless Our Noble King." The crowd rose to its feet when it was played and it started a tradition that continues to this day.

In 1747 the great actor David Garrick became manager of the Drury Lane. Many of his greatest triumphs occurred on its stage. The Adams brothers made more alterations to the interior in 1775 and finished them just in time to open the managership of Richard Brinsley Sheridan with his new play—*The School for Scandal*. John Philip Kemble took over the reins in 1788, but the Drury Lane's fortunes began to decline. The grand old place was finally razed in 1791 after an honorable life of almost 100 years.

The third Drury Lane was a monster of 3611 seats designed by Sir Henry Holland. It opened in 1794 with Sheridan back in the manager's position and John Philip Kemble and his sister Sarah Siddons as leading performers. Keeping a sad tradition alive, George III was shot in the building by a mad gunman in 1800. As usual one of the great concerns for theatres at this time was fire. The third Drury Lane had an iron safety curtain installed and also had huge water tanks aloft to quench potential conflagrations. All of this was to no avail and it burned to the ground in 1809. The story is told that Sheridan sat at a local coffee house that evening and when queried about the blaze quipped wryly, "A man may surely be allowed to take a glass of wine by his own fireside."

Drury Lane Number Four, which opened in 1812, stands before you as the oldest operating theatre in London. It was designed by the architect Benjamin Wyatt and currently seats 2226 people. The prologue on the opening night was written by Lord Byron. In its early years it saw some of the great successes by Edmund Kean. Gas lighting was added in 1817 to compete with Covent Garden. The classical portico was added in 1820 and the side colonnade on Russell Street was put in place in 1826. The pillars came from the demolition of part of John Nash's quadrant in Regent Street.

Charles Macready took over as manager in 1841. The theatre was refurbished and attained new eminence as the premier hall for large scale spectacles, operas, and melodramas. Utilizing its large elevator stage sections and giant treadmills, there were boat races, horse races, and Ben Hur-style chariot races. Scenic displays featured events like Piccadilly Circus at midnight in a blizzard, a full scale Zulu war, and Bank Holiday weekend at Hampstead Heath.

**12**

In 1915 cinema took over for a spell and the D. W. Griffith epics *Birth of a Nation* and *Intolerance* played there. A major interior remodeling occurred in 1921. The domed rotunda and the entrance staircases are now the only remaining features of Wyatt's original Georgian design. The house continued as a venue for musicals and reviews and continued to function throughout the second world war even though somewhat damaged by bombs. The post-war years saw a long string of American musicals inluding *Oklahoma, Carousel, South Pacific,* and *The King and I.* In 1958 *My Fair Lady* arrived and stayed for six years, a record surpassed by *Miss Saigon.*

*It's now time to inspect the building a bit more closely. Enter the lobby and look around, if only to see the **Shakespeare statue**. You may also wish to check for tickets. Drury Lane seats do not normally show up at the half price ticket booth.*

*When you leave the lobby to go outside again, turn right and walk toward the corner. The bust in the memorial on the wall is of **Augustus Harris** the manager of Drury Lane from 1879-1896. From the busy corner take a left for about fifty paces down **Russell Street** and then a right into **Bow Street**. As you're doing this you may notice the signs for the Theatre Museum across the way. Don't panic. We'll be back to this spot after we circle around and through Covent Garden.*

**Drury Lane's Shakespeare statue**

*The corner of Bow and Russell has been a lynchpin of London's arts and cultural activities for at least 200 years. Two of its greatest theatres are in sight and as you look down Russell Street toward the old Covent Garden market buildings, it should take little imagination to see instead of today's busy restaurants the most important coffee houses of the 17th and 18th centuries. Will's Coffee House was right on the corner.* John Dryden was its leading customer for forty years. Samuel Pepys saw him there in 1664 ". . . with all the wits in town." Will's was also the favorite spot of the poet, Alexander Pope, who was introduced to the local wags by Covent Garden resident and playwright William Wycherley. *Opposite Will's was Button's Coffee House.* Joseph Addison was the reigning genius there. *Also in this street were Tom's Coffee House (a hangout for Sam Johnson, Henry Fielding, Joshua Reynolds, Colley Cibber, Oliver Goldsmith, and David Garrick) and Davies' Bookshop (Thomas Davies, prop.) where James Boswell met Dr. Johnson.*

*For now walk forward on Bow Street. John Rich (1682-1761), actor manager of Lincoln's Inn Theatre and builder of the first Covent Garden Theatre, lived nearby. The novelist Henry Fielding lived in the fourth house from Russell Street from 1707-54 and the actress Peg Woffington had lodgings in the 6th house from the corner for forty years—from 1720 to 1760. The actors Charles Macklin and David Garrick occasionally*

**12**

**Memorial to Augustus Harris**

*shared that residence with her. You'll shortly, on your right, come to the cozy* **Globe Pub.** *Its walls are lined with celebrity pictures and some nice theatre prints.*

*Across the street from the pub used to stand the green and white cast-iron tracery of the Floral Hall, once a flower market and then a scenery dock for the Royal Opera House; it has now been swallowed up as a part of the Covent Garden expansion. Somewhere between the Floral Hall and the Opera House lived the well known Restoration playwright William Wycherley. And not far from where you're standing on the right hand side of the street was the infamous Cock tavern.* According to the stories, Wycherley's wife would allow him to go there only because it was close by and she could keep an eye on him. In 1663 at the Cock Tavern three courtiers got drunk, went out on the balcony, removed their clothes, and proceeded to harangue the public. The crowd below was not amused and the young men were arrested. Luckily for them, Charles II found their episode amusing and came forward to pay their fines.

*Had that episode occurred eighty years later, the young ruffians would not have had far to go for their hearing. A few more steps on is the Bow Street Police Station.* In 1748 this was the site of the Bow Street Police Court. The first magistrate of that court was area resident Henry Fielding. To assist in keeping control of what was one of the most raucous districts in town, Fielding created a corps of fit and speedy detectives who became known as the Bow Street Runners. The buttons of their uniforms were made of copper and thereby goes another name for the constabulary that has stuck through the years.

*Let's turn our attention now from police matters to the grandiose white portico of the* **Royal Opera House** *or the Covent Garden Theatre. Theatregoers have been beating a steady path to this same plot of ground for more than 250 years.*

The first theatre on the site, dating from 1732, was an 1800-seat house known as the Theatre Royal Covent Garden. It was royal because it was in the direct line of succession for one of the two exclusive theatre patents awarded by Charles II. Covent Garden's patent

**12**

**Royal
Opera
House**

came to manager John Rich via Sir Charles Davenant's Dukes Theatre
at Dorset Garden (Walk Five). The other patent, as we just mentioned,
resides with the Drury Lane Theatre and you actually can see it if
you tour the building.

The architect for the first Theatre Royal was E. Shepherd. The ever
cantankerous and litigious John Rich was the manager. At one point
in his career he killed a fellow actor in a fight over a wig. A more joy-
ful highlight of those early years is that the inaugural performance of
Handel's oratorio *The Messiah* took place here in 1744. Other historic
productions were the first performances of Sheridan's *The Rivals,* and
Oliver Goldsmith's *She Stoops to Conquer.* The first theatre was renovated in both 1784 and 1791. Then in 1807 it burned to the ground.

The second Covent Garden (1808) was modeled after the Temple
of Minerva on the Acropolis and designed by the neoclassical architect Robert Smirke. Robert Flaxman contributed some grand exterior bas-reliefs. The interior and the stage epitomized the 19th century
desire for scenic spectacle. The seating capacity was around 3000 and

**12**

the proscenium opening was 43 feet wide and 38 feet high. The stage itself was 85 feet wide and 92 feet deep. Technical theatre history was made here as well. It was the first theatre to be lit by gaslight in 1817 and also the first building in which an early version of the follow spotlight was used in 1837. A pressured flame was focused on a block of lime that burned brightly at the single point of intense heat. This point of bright light was then focusable with a set of lenses. As you may have guessed, it was called a "limelight" and hence our phrase "in the limelight."

The first manager of the second theatre was John Philip Kemble, whom we mentioned a few pages ago as the man who got in trouble when he tried to raise prices to pay for the new building and set off the so called Old Price riots. All of the great actors of the 19th century played at the second Theatre Royal. Edmund Kean is perhaps best remembered for his final exit. He collapsed in March of 1833 while playing Othello to his son Charles' Iago. As he fell into his son's arms he is said to have cried out, "Oh God! I am dying . . . speak to them for me." The actor William Charles Macready, well known for his new emphasis on historical costuming, became manager in 1837; he was followed by the remarkable Madame Vestris, who pioneered the development of the box set. You can see in the history of this theatre quite clearly how the invention of better lighting instruments between 1817 to 1850 seems to have led to more attention to costume and three-dimensional scenic detail. Once producers and audiences could see the stage more clearly, they seemed to demand more and better things to see.

Fire returned to the site again in 1856, leaving, as many contemporary prints showed, a smoking shell. The third Covent Garden, known then as the Royal Italian Opera House and now as the Royal Opera House, was opened in 1858. Sir James Barry, the architect, produced a Roman Renaissance building with a magnificent raised Corinthian portico. The statues on either side of the facade and the Flaxman bas-reliefs from the previous building were reused.

The 19th century building became increasingly inadequate to meet the demands of modern stagings of opera and ballet, so in the early 1990s a major redesign was projected to bring it into the 21st century. A controversial Lottery grant of £78 million enabled the work to begin, despite a storm of protest from the press, politicians, non-patrons of opera and ballet, and other disappointed arts practitioners; and by 1998 the Royal Opera House had become a huge building site. When the work is finished, it is hoped by the dawn of the Millennium, the old Floral Hall building will have been absorbed into the backstage area to provide for the first time adequate rehearsal space, scenery workshops and storage, and all the myriad support operations that are needed to keep modern opera and ballet productions running smoothly.

The auditorium will preserve its traditional horseshoe shape, but

**12**

seating and sightlines will be improved. In 1998 Placido Domingo weighed into the acrimonious debate about seat pricing, threatening not to return to its stage unless more cheap tickets were available than in the past. The management of the whole rebuilding operation has been fraught with problems, resignations and dismissals; but so much money and prestige has now been committed that it seems certain that the doors of the Royal Opera House will be thrown open again by the beginning of the next century. Until then there is little to see except the aerial ballet of huge cranes to the accompaniment of a rhythmic chorus of pneumatic drills.

*When you reach the back of the theatre on James Street, turn left toward the old Covent Garden Market buildings; jog right as you near the piazza and look left for the classical portico of the church known as* **St. Paul's Covent Garden.**

This may be the time to make some general comments on Covent Garden. Refer to the bibliography if you wish to pursue the history of this remarkable area in more depth. For the moment it should suffice that you know that the general area you are now in was originally a garden that belonged to the Convent of St. Peter at Westminster Abbey—hence Convent Garden and finally Covent Garden. The land was ceded to the Russell family by the crown in 1541 as a part of the widespread re-distribution of religious holdings after the Reformation.

Francis Russell, the fourth Earl of Bedford, wanted to develop the estate further and in the 1630s work began under the architectural supervision of Inigo Jones, who was a consummate theatre artist as well as the King's favorite architect. Jones was responsible for bringing the concept of painted perspective scenery to England from Italy and designed splendid costumes and scenery for the Court Masques written by Ben Jonson in the early 1600s. His fascinating but unbuilt design for a 17th century theatre is being constructed as a part of the Globe Theatre project on Bankside.

Jones also brought visions of neo-classic architecture and Italian town planning back from his continental visits, and his design for Covent Garden incorporated a large piazza, houses with open arcades, a stretch of the Duke of Bedford's own gardens, and a church.

The square, when completed, began to attract market traders and over the years became the central fruit, vegetable, and flower market in London. In the 1830s special cast-iron market buildings were constructed. Growth, congestion, and transportation difficulties sounded the death knell for the Covent Garden that Londoners had known for two hundred years. In 1974 the markets were relocated to suburban Nine Elms and the old buildings were redeveloped into the bustling shopping and entertainment mecca you see today. Covent Garden remains alive and very well.

*Let's focus now on the church that was designed as the architectural anchor for the piazza— St. Paul's Covent Garden.* The story is often

**12**

**St. Paul's Covent Garden**

told that the Duke of Bedford was a frugal man and not too keen about ecclesiastical ostentation. He emphasized to Inigo Jones, the architect, that he "wou'd not have it much better than a barn." To which Jones replied, "Well then, you shall have the handsomest barn in England."

*The Tuscan portico you are looking at is clearly handsome and was obviously intended to be the entrance to the church. But the church authorities insisted that the altar be located at the east end of the sanctuary and thus the apparent front door is only a bit of theatrical magic.* This is an amusing little irony as St. Paul's Covent Garden has become known as the Actors Church. The theatre is a profession built on artifice and its members have long accustomed themselves to entering

**12**

The rear entrance to St. Paul's Covent Garden

196

their hallowed performance ground by the back or stage door.

Think also of this portico as a true stage set. On May 9, 1662 Samuel Pepys recorded in his diary that he saw a *Punch and Judy* show under it. He enjoyed it so much that he brought his wife back two weeks later. If you are lucky enough to be here in May, you may have a chance to see the remarkable puppeteer's service that is a part of the Maye Faire. During that time the entire garden outside is full of Punch and Judy shows and booths where you can buy puppets, theatres, costumes, and other craft items; but throughout the year you can watch buskers, fire-eaters, jugglers and other entertainers here. When it rains they can be found performing inside the covered Market shopping area.

You are also looking at the opening scene of George Bernard Shaw's *Pygmalion* and its musical namesake *My Fair Lady*. Liza Doolittle is a Covent Garden flower girl and she meets her Henry Higgins underneath the portico of St. Paul's Covent Garden. It remains today the central buskers' platform for Covent Garden and continues to provide a theatrical backdrop for the mimes, comedians, and musicians who now frequent the area from morning till night.

*After looking at the portico, move forward and to your right around the block that contains the church. You should find yourself on* **King Street** *and moving away from the market. Nicolas Rowe (1674-1718), a minor playwright and poet laureate of England, had lodgings on this street. David Garrick lived briefly at Number 27. Thomas Arne, the composer and main music director at the Drury Lane, was born on the street at Number 31. Number 35 was the original home of the Garrick Club.*

*When you reach Bedford Street, make a left and then another quick left through the gates and into the path that will take you to the* **real entrance of St. Paul's.** *You'll find a delightful, flower filled garden/park.* Not one in a thousand of the hordes of tourists descending in a feeding frenzy on Covent Garden today will find this spot. And speaking of frenzy, if you want a deliciously creepy picture of Covent Garden as it was in the old vegetable market days, rent a copy of Alfred Hitchcock's classic film *Frenzy*. It takes place in and around the Covent Garden area.

Rest a bit on a bench if you wish and then enter the church, which is normally open from 9 to 4 Monday through Friday and for services on Sunday. Bear in mind that what you see inside is a reconstruction. The building burned in 1795 and was rebuilt to Inigo Jones' design. It was remodeled again in 1871. Wander to your heart's content. There is often a friendly parishioner around to answer questions. The church's long connection with the arts and actors is displayed throughout. Remember that both Drury Lane and the Royal Opera House have been in the parish since the 18th century.

Buried here are William Wycherley, Charles Macklin, and Thomas Arne, the composer of both "God Save the Queen" and "Rule Britannia."

**12**

The most moving tomb is that of the actress Ellen Terry. The silver urn containing her ashes is kept in a niche in the south wall. The church today is often the site for memorial services for members of the theatrical profession, and handsome wooden plaques commemorate a host of more contemporary performers.

*Leave St. Paul's via your entry path. Upon reaching **Bedford Street**, turn left. Stop briefly at the **Henrietta Street** intersection.* Richard Brinsley Sheridan fought his third duel here with a certain Captain Matthew over a remark made by the Captain about Sheridan's beloved Miss Elizabeth Linley. *Continue on Bedford Street one more block to **Maiden Lane** and then turn left. You will pass the famous theatrical restaurant Rules and then shortly be back to the market area of Covent Garden. The Jubilee Market on your right is a glorified flea and food market. Ahead of you and to your left are the more upscale central market shops and restaurants.*

*There is theatre everywhere in the refurbished market halls, but only one spot that you must visit. In the South Hall (upstairs) is the tiny little Benjamin Pollock Toy Shop, an offshoot of the Pollock Toy Museum on Scala Street, and they have a nice collection of Toy Theatres, Punch and Judy paraphernalia, and other theatre memorabilia.* If you are not familiar with the Toy Theatre movement, this visit might encourage you to visit Pollock's original Toy Museum at a later date. (See the Unstrung Pearls section at the end of the walks for more information.)

*When you are finished in the market, proceed to the side opposite St. Paul's church. The Floral Hall and the Royal Opera House are on your left and the **London Transport Museum** is on your right. Dead ahead of you, beyond the barriers that keep the traffic out, is Russell Street. Walk toward it and you should have no trouble identifying on your right the entrance to the **Theatre Museum**. Enter and enjoy. The Museum holds both permanent and seasonal exhibitions of all kinds of theatrical memorabilia, conducts workshops in all aspects of theatre work, has a regular lecture program, and stages readings and occasional productions. You need to make an appointment in advance to use the research facilities of the Study Room in the basement, and spaces are normally limited to professional researchers and writers in theatre history. One little hint. Make sure you look at all the famous handprints as you go down the entrance ramp and do hit the loos before you leave. The Shakespeare tiles are well worth seeing even if you don't need to use the facilities.*

*The nearest Tube station to the Theatre Museum is the **Covent Garden Station** on the Piccadilly Line. We have pointed it out a couple of times already. To find it from the Theatre Museum turn left as you exit and return to the market area via Russell Street then curve around to your right until you find James Street leading up out of the market. If you run into King Street or the church again, you've gone too far; turn around and go back. Move up James Street and shortly you'll reach Long Acre; the friendly blue and red circle of London Transport will be on your left.*

**12**

**Left: Floral Hall**

**Below: Theatre Museum**

**12**

# WALK THIRTEEN

❁

# THE OLD VIC
## TO THE
## NATIONAL
## THEATRE
## AND THE
## SOUTH BANK

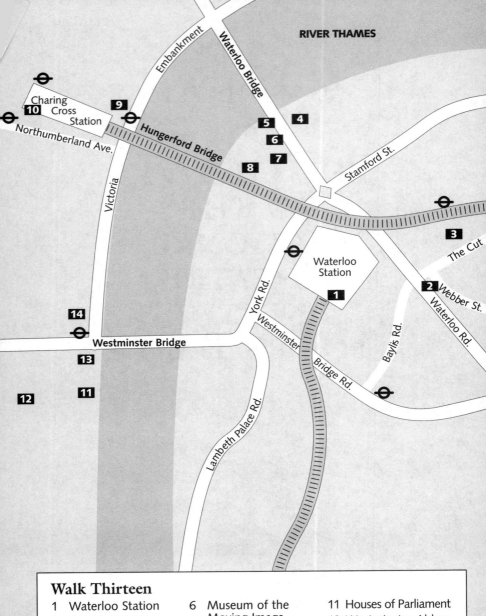

**RIVER THAMES**

## Walk Thirteen

1 Waterloo Station
2 Old Vic Theatre
3 Young Vic Theatre
4 Royal National Theatre
5 National Film Theatre
6 Museum of the Moving Image
7 Hayward Gallery
8 Royal Festival Hall
9 Embankment Tube Station
10 Charing Cross Station
11 Houses of Parliament
12 Westminster Abbey
13 Big Ben
14 Westminster Tube Station

**STARTING POINT:** Waterloo Underground Station (Bakerloo or Northern Line).

**APPROXIMATE TIME:** Less than an hour in actual walking time, but half a day if you take full advantage of the opportunities to tour and browse.

T*his walk traces the growth of the National Theatre from its spiritual home in the Old Vic, which became its first official base, before it moved to the cultural complex on the South Bank of the Thames.*

O*ur starting point is* **Waterloo Station.** *Follow the exit signs to* **Waterloo Road** *and the* **Old Vic Theatre.** *Turn right out of the station exit and walk for about 125 yards to the* **Baylis Road** *junction. As you walk you will see ahead to the left the facade of the Old Vic, at the beginning of the road named* **The Cut.** *Cross in front of it and turn right into* **Webber Street,** *where you will find immediately a plaque on the wall recording that the first stone was laid on the 14th day of September, 1816, by the Prince of Saxe Coburg and HRH the Princess Charlotte of Wales.* She was the Prince Regent's only daughter and heir-presumptive to the throne, but by the time the new Royal Coburg Theatre opened its doors in 1818, she had died in childbirth. In 1833 it was renamed the Victoria Theatre after the 14-year-old Princess Victoria, who visited it that year with her mother, but never returned as Queen. This is hardly surprising, as the neighbourhood soon be-

Waterloo Station

13

203

**Emma Cons plaque**

came a byword for deprivation and depravity, and the standards of the theatre program declined accordingly, to what was described by one journalist in the 1840s as "the most degraded in London," and another said its productions were "fit for an audience of felons."

Its transformation was begun in 1880 by Emma Cons, whose motivation was more moral than theatrical. She and some wealthy philanthropic backers set out to combat the evils of alcohol by reopening it as the Royal Victoria Coffee and Music Hall. Since it was not licensed to present plays either, its repertoire consisted of variety acts, musical concerts, and later opera, interspersed with lectures and temperance meetings. When Miss Cons died in 1912, she passed on the management of the Victoria Hall to her niece, Lilian Baylis, who had been her assistant since 1898.

Miss Baylis immediately obtained a theatre license from the Lord Chamberlain, and the first Shakespearean productions were presented in the spring of 1914. The Victorian Hall had staggered from one financial crisis to another ever since 1880, but the outbreak of war was to prove its salvation. While the commercial managements of the West End turned to light escapist fare, Lilian Baylis offered a season of combined opera and Shakespeare from October 1914 until the end of April 1915—16 operas and 16 plays in less than thirty weeks.

**Lilan Baylis, by Miss Cecil Leslie**
Reprinted with permission
of the National Portrait Gallery

Over the next decade and a half, under the direction of men like Ben Greet, Robert Atkins and Harcourt Williams, and with the drawing-power of actresses like Sybil Thorndike and Edith Evans, what had now become known as the Old Vic built up a loyal following. It was John Gielgud's arrival in 1929 to lead the company which brought new audiences flocking across the Thames to see him in several parts, most notably as Richard II and Hamlet. The following year Ralph Richardson joined him, and soon anyone with ambitions to be taken seriously as a classical actor wanted to make their mark here. The roll-call in the

**13**

**The Old Vic**

Thirties included Peggy Ashcroft, Laurence Olivier, Alec Guinness, Michael Redgrave, Flora Robson, and Charles Laughton.

On the death of Lilian Baylis in 1937, Tyrone Guthrie took over the reins of the company, and when the theatre was bombed in 1941 he kept the Old Vic flag flying in the provinces. In 1943 Ralph Richardson and Laurence Olivier were released from the Navy to become co-directors of the Old Vic Company at the New Theatre— those productions have gone down into theatrical legend.

The building was reopened in 1950, and in an ambitious Five Year Plan Michael Benthall presented the entire Shakespearean canon. In 1962, the Old Vic seemed the natural choice as the temporary home of the National Theatre under its first Director, Laurence Olivier. Now the Waterloo Road became the first stop for all theatre lovers. When the National moved into its purpose-built South Bank site in 1974, the Old Vic began another period of uncertainty, until the Toronto-based impresario, Ed Mirvish, bought it and pumped millions into refurbishing it and supporting several different companies. In 1997 the Peter Hall Company launched an ambitious repertoire of classics and new plays running seven nights a week, but at the end of that year the Mirvish family finally decided to cut their losses and return to Canada. So in 1998, one of the most famous landmarks in the 20th century history of British drama went dark, but it seems inconceivable that it should be allowed ever to join the sad list of Lost London Theatres; we can only hope that by the time of your visit the Old

**13**

**Young Vic**

Vic baton will have been picked up by a worthy successor to the names mentioned above.

*Now walk further along The Cut for 200 yards, until you reach the Young Vic on the left hand side of the road.* This junior branch was opened by Dame Sybil Thorndike on 12 August, 1970, to double as a young people's theatre and a studio for the National Theatre Company. In 1974 it, too, became independent of the National Theatre, and now hosts a mixture of its own productions and some from the Royal Shakespeare Company. Its current prospects seem more secure than those of its original parent just up the road.

*Retrace your steps along **The Cut**, and turn right into **Waterloo Road**. Walk past the entrance to **Waterloo Station** until you reach the large roundabout at the end. Descend to the underpass and follow the signs to **Waterloo Bridge**. As you emerge onto it you will see immediately on your right steps leading down to what has now been renamed the **Royal National Theatre**. The rebuilding works completed in 1998 have opened up the river frontage to make it more welcoming and accessible. (On your way to the National, if you have the sudden urge to take off for Paris instead, you're in luck. The entrance to the Chunnel terminal is on your left.)*

**Chunnel entrance**

**13**

The foyers of the National, where the attractions include exhibitions, a particularly good theatre bookshop, bars and restaurants where you can enjoy a coffee, snack or full meal, are open from 10 AM to 11 PM. Before the evening performances there is free music in the Lyttelton foyer on the ground floor, and frequent platform performances in the three auditoria—talks, interviews or discussions at modest prices. You may book a backstage tour during the day at the Information Desk, and purchase seats for that day's performances at the Box Office. (The daily allocation goes quickly, so join the queue early).

The history of the opening of the building was in sharp contrast to its smooth running today. A less resilient director than Sir Peter Hall, who succeeded Olivier, would have had a nervous breakdown from the succession of building delays, union obstructionism, and political and press attacks that attended that long drawn out saga in the mid-1970s. In desperation the Company started giving open-air performances on the Lilian Baylis Terrace overlooking the river, to herald their arrival on the South Bank. At the first acoustic test on the Lyttelton Stage Albert Finney could not resist the temptation to frighten the assembled gathering by mutely mouthing his lines, and only when their faces went white did he break the silence with his normal voice. (For the full story of this troubled period read *Peter Hall's Diaries, 1972-80*).

The first three directors each made a massive contribution towards the creation and maintenance of the National as the best as well as the most important theatre in the land. Sir Laurence Olivier launched it into orbit at the Old Vic, Sir Peter Hall brought it safely into its berth at the South Bank, and Richard Eyre consolidated its reputation with an astonishing success rate (recognized by the award of his knighthood at the end of his term there). In 1998 he handed over to Trevor Nunn, whose track record at the RSC and elsewhere would indicate that he too is a man of theatrical vision as well as a very safe pair of hands.

*If your walk began early in the morning you could end your visit by lunching at the National, but if the sun is shining you would enjoy a stroll along the bank of the Thames to one of the other possibilities for refreshment of mind and body. Turn left out of the Theatre and under Waterloo Bridge you will pass the cafe of the National Film Theatre; behind it lies the **Museum of the Moving Image**. A few paces after you emerge from under the bridge you will see the steps up to the **Hayward Gallery**, which houses some of the most stimulating art exhibitions to be found in the metropolis. Next come the small and medium-sized concert halls, the Purcell Room and the Queen Elizabeth Hall. Your destination is the next building — the **Royal Festival Hall**, which is usually just as lively during the day as the National Theatre. The RFH has bars and restaurants on several floors, with live music at lunchtimes, busy record and book shops,*

**13**

**13**

**Scenes from the National Theatre: exterior, bookshop, and restaurant**

**Top: Royal Festival Hall**
**Bottom: Museum of the Moving Image**

and events that range from music in the large concert hall to literary debates and discussions in the small Voice Box upstairs.

To end this walk now, the quickest route is to walk to the back of the Festival Hall and follow the signs to **Waterloo Tube Station**. A more attractive conclusion is to cross the Thames by the footbridge alongside Hungerford Railway Bridge, which brings you to either Embankment or Charing Cross Stations. But if there is still spring in your step then continue along the South Bank to **Westminster Bridge** and walk over it to the Houses of Parliament. If they are sitting you could queue to watch

**13**

*the daily drama in either House; if not then continue across Parliament Square to Westminster Abbey. This is the setting for the Memorial Services of the greatest actors — Sir Henry Irving, Sir Ralph Richardson, Lord Olivier, Dame Peggy Ashcroft — and Poet's Corner is now so full of plaques and busts that in 1997 Oscar Wilde was commemorated by a stained-glass window, unveiled by Sir John Gielgud at a ceremony attended by many leading actors and writers. Then return to Westminster Bridge, where you will find the* **Westminster Tube Station** *at the foot of the* **Big Ben clocktower.***

❁

# UNSTRUNG
# PEARLS

❁

N o matter how you string individual pearls, there are always a few that will not fit conveniently on any strand. They are either too modest, too specialized, or simply too far off a planned route to allow for easy inclusion. Other leftovers are just so large or important that they seem to call for an unencumbered visit of their own. Here then, in a rough order of importance, is a final list of not-to-be-missed theatrical pearls.

**1. THE VICTORIA AND ALBERT MUSEUM:** Exhibition Road and Cromwell Gardens SW 10, (South Kensington tube station). Take the tunnel that starts right in the tube station and follow the signs. This is the national museum of fine and applied art and any theatre lover with a technical or design interest will glory in the decorative objects, the furniture collections, the fabrics, and especially the costume court.

**2. THE NATIONAL GALLERY: Trafalgar Square** and **THE TATE GALLERY: Millbank** are London's two major world class art galleries. They are not specifically theatrical, but they are two of London's general jewels and all visitors with any kind of arts sensitivity should have them high on their priority list.

**3. SAMUEL FRENCH'S THEATRE BOOKSHOP:** 52 Fitzroy Street W1 (Warren Street tube). It was for many years, when it was located in an enchanting old building just off Covent Garden, London's preeminent theatre bookstore. It now has several competitors, but is still top notch. A visit here makes a nice pairing with #4, Pollock's Toy Museum. They are quite close together.

**4. POLLOCK'S TOY MUSEUM:** 1 Scala Street, W1 (Goodge Street tube) For devotees of Punch and Judy and the charming 19th century Toy Theatre movement, this little museum is a treasure and a must.

**5. THE BANQUETING HOUSE:** Whitehall SW1 (Charing Cross tube) Inigo Jones designed the hall, Rubens painted the ceiling, and Charles I took his last walk from here out on to the scaffold before a large and silent crowd. The whole building reeks of history. This is a general tourist destination, but as a theatre buff you are obligated to go if only to imagine the sumptuous Court Masques that were staged there by Inigo Jones and Ben Jonson.

*Those are the five final pearls. Walk in peace and above all care for this beautiful city. London, like Shakespeare, is for all time and all peoples, but it's truly special for those who hold a love of the art of live theatre in their hearts.*

# SELECTED BIBLIOGRAPHY

Adcock, A. St. John. *Famous Houses and Literary Shrines of London*. New York: Barnes and Noble, 1993.

Arnold, Wendy. *The Historic Hotels of London*. London: Owl Books, 1987.

Ash, Russell. *The Londoner's Almanac*. London: Century Publishing, 1985.

Bergan, Ronald. *The Great Theatres of London*. San Francisco: Chronicle Books, 1988.

Borer, Mary Cathcart. *Covent Garden*. London: Abelard-Schuman Ltd., 1967

Brockett, Oscar. *History of the Theatre*. New York: Alleyn and Bacon, 1995.

Chambers, Michael. *London The Secret City*. London: Ocean Books n.d.

Clunn, Harold P. *The Face of London*. London: Simpkin Marshall, Ltd., 1982.

Connell, Charles. *They Gave Us Shakespeare*. Stocksfield: The Oriel Press, 1982.

Cottrell, John. *Laurence Olivier*. London: Hodder and Stoughton Coronet Edition, 1977.

Day, Barry. *This Wooden "O":Shakespeare's Globe Restored*. London: Oberon Books, 1996.

Edwards, Christopher ed. *The London Theatre Guide 1576-1642*. London: The Burlington Press Ltd., 1979.

Fairfield, Sheila. *The Streets of London*. London: Macmillan Publishers Ltd., 1984.

Fay, Stephen. *Power Play: The Life and Times of Peter Hall*. London: Hodder and Stoughton, 1995

French, Ylva ed. *The Blue Guide London*. London: A&C Black, 1998.

Gardner, Douglas. *The Covent Garden Guide*. London: Ernest Benn Ltd., 1980.

Goodwin, John ed. *Peter Hall's Diaries*. New York: Harper and Row, 1984.

Gray, Robert. *A History of London*. New York: Taplinger Publishing Company, 1978.

Halliday, F. E. *Shakespeare*. New York: Thomas Yoseloff, 1961.

Hartnoll, Phyllis ed. *The Oxford Companion to the Theatre*. Oxford: Oxford University Press, 1972.

Jackson, Peter. *Walks in Old London*. New York: Barnes and Noble, 1995.

Jenner, Michael. *London Heritage*. London: Michael Joseph Ltd., 1988.

Jones, Edward and Woodward, Christopher. *A Guide to the Architecture of London*. New York: Thames and Hudson, 1992.

Kempson, Rachel, Lady Redgrave. *Life Among the Redgraves*. New York, E.P. Dutton, 1986.

Kendall, Alan. *David Garrick: A Biography*. London: Harrap Ltd., 1985.

Kimball, George. *The Pocket Guide to London Theatre*. Topsfield, MA: Salen House Publishers, 1987.

MacGregor-Hastie, Roy. *Nell Gwyn*. London: Robert Hale, 1987.

Mac Queen-Pope, Walter. *Ghosts and Greasepaint*. London: R. Hale, 1951.

Mander, Raymond and Mitchenson, Joe. *The Theatres of London*. London: New English Library, 1975.

Mander, Raymond and Mitchenson, Joe. *The Lost Theatres of London*. Rupert Hart-Davis, 1968.

Marowitz, Charles ed.. *The Encore Reader*. London: Methuen and Company Ltd., 1965.

Mee, Arthur. *London: The City and Westminster*. London: Hodder and Stoughton, 1975.

Morton, Brian. *Americans in London*. New York: William Morrow, 1986.

Nicholson, Robert. *London Guide*. London: Robert Nicholson Publications, Ltd., 1990.

Ousby, Ian. *Blue Guide Literary Britain and Ireland*. London: A.C. Black Limited, 1985.

Rasmusen, Steen Eiler. *London the Unique City*. Cambridge, MA.: The MIT Press, (revised edition) 1982.

Richards, Timothy M. and Curt, James Stevens. *City of London Pubs*. Newton Abbot: David and Charles Ltd., 1973.

Roberts, Howard and Godfrey, Walter H., eds. *London County Council Survey of London: Bankside*. Vol. XXII. London: London County Council, 1950.

Rodgers, Malcolm. *Blue Guide Museums and Galleries of London*. London: Ernest Benn Ltd., 1983

Room, Adrian. *Dictionary of Britain*. London: Oxford University Press, 1986.

Rosenthal, Harold. *Covent Garden: Memories and Traditions*. London: Michael Joseph Ltd, 1976.

Rossiter, Stuwart ed. *Blue Guide London*. London: Ernest Benn Ltd., 1983.

Rossi, Alfred ed. *Astonish Us in the Morning: Tyrone Guthrie Remembered*. London: Hutchinson and Company, 1977.

Rumbelow, Donald. *The Triple Tree: Newgate, Tyburn, and Old Bailey*.

Sampson, Anthony. *The Changing Anatomy of Britian*. New York: Random House, 1982.

Sanderson, Michael. *From Irving to Olivier*. London: Athlone Press, 1984.

Saunders, Ann. *The Art and Architecture of London*. Oxford: Phaidon Press Ltd., 1984.

Smith, Irwin. *Shakespeare's Blackfriars Theatre*

Speaight, Robert. *Shakespeare: The Man and His Achievement*. London: J. M. Dent and Sons, Ltd., 1977.

Thorne, Robert. *Covent Garden Market*. London: The Architectural Press, 1980.

Tunstall, Brian. *The Pictorial History of Southwark Cathedral*. London: Pitkin Pictorials Ltd., 1967.

Williams, George C. *Guide to Literary London*. London, B.T. Batsford Ltd., 1973.

Wittich, John. *Discovering London's Inns and Taverns*. London: Shire Publications Ltd., 1978.

# INDEX